MW01591976

True Stories of My Life

by Ferenc Baba

DORRANCE
PUBLISHING CO
EST. 1920
PITTSBURGH, PENNSYLVANIA 15238

Dorrance Publishing Co
585 Alpha Drive
Suite 103
Pittsburgh, PA 15238
Visit our website at *www.dorrancebookstore.com*

ISBN: 978-1-4809-5647-6
eISBN: 978-1-4809-5624-7

Introduction

Hi, my name is Ferenc Baba. I was born in a small village in Hungary. I decided to write this story to help people recognize a healing process.

Rejection was handed to me at birth. I worked hard with no appreciation or parental support. I worked hard and learned as much as I could to make a strong foundation to build a successful life. Specifically, I learned to be an auto mechanic, electrician, and construction worker. If anything came up in my life that I didn't know how to do, I bought a book and educated myself to finish any job. I came to have lots of talent and skill. Afterwards, I was able to assist many people who needed help.

For about five years, I thought about writing this book. My story is about my life in Hungary and the United States. My lifestyle has been deeply affected by how I was raised in Hungary. My mother blamed me for everything in our house and family.

From as far back as I can remember, this blaming of one child grew in my heart. I accepted it as a basic truth. This way of discipline/communication was all I knew.

My mother must be right because she is my mother. I love her. She did her best.

Purpose

To heal those in my family, including myself, and reach out to others who may be faced with similar struggles. Read this to discover the rest of my story and help you if you have similar problems.

Chapter 1
About My Parents

My mother came from a very poor family, and my father came from a very wealthy family. Her mother died when she was two years old and her father died when she was five; not only poor, but now also an orphan. Her brother raised her for about two years and then sold her to a rich family when she was about seven years old. When she was about eight years old, she was forced to climb a tree to shake off fruit for the hogs. She fell out of the tree and severely injured her hip. She was never taken to the doctor; she limped her whole life.

When she was twelve years and eight months old, the rich man raped her. Because she was pregnant, the rich man beat her badly. This happened inside a barn, and the rich man assumed she died. In the 1940s, slaves had no value in my country. The rich man had money to buy another slave. A farm dog stayed with my wounded mother. The man did not check to see if she had died or not. The farm dog protected her.

My father came to the rich man's farm to deliver parts for a tractor. While working close to the barn, my father heard a noise and went inside the barn to investigate what was making this strange sound. The dog growled at my father. Within a short time, the dog sensed my father's good intentions. The dog knew this man would help the wounded lady. The dog let my father come close to my mother.

My father picked her up from the ground and carried her to his Model T Ford. He rescued my mother without telling the rich man of his plans. My father took my mother and the dog home. Of course, she lost the baby. The rich man broke her shoulder and ribs; she was lucky there was no damage to her lungs.

After my mother survived, my father kept her as a slave. His wife became ill. She took care of his wife and their two children. After three years, his wife died. My mother continued caring for the two children and helping my father on the farm.

My mother turned eighteen, and then became pregnant from my father. They were not married because he was not allowed to marry a poor girl. Their first child was a boy, born on March 12, 1945. Their second child was also a boy, born on August 23, 1947. My mother continued to raise my father's two children and her two children.

Then, my mother and father had a twenty-three-year age difference. My father's family didn't want him to marry to this poor girl either. They called her "the slave". My father called her "a caretaker". But in my country, caretaker was not correct. She was a slave. She needed to please and work hard for my father.

My father and mother finally got married in 1954, since there was a change in the law. The reason my father had two children to prove to the family, even though she was a slave and poor, she was a very honest and hard-working person.

Her dream was to someday have a daughter. Then she took a chance with my father, without even being married, with a third pregnancy. She had a dream she would probably have a girl. At that time, a few times it happened that finally someone would have twins. Especially while pregnant, she was overweight and could not run over to a doctor. Even when somebody became pregnant and waited for nine months to deliver that baby, there was not a checkup every month, and how the woman felt did not really matter. If pregnant, a woman should wait nine months, deliver it, and not make a big deal of the pregnancy, especially if she was not a part of a family.

So, my mother went in May of 1950 to the hospital, even though she was just seven and a half months pregnant. But complications came up and she delivered me and my sister at seven and a half months. I was born first, and my mother asked for a doctor. "She's a girl?"

And the doctor said, "No, no, no."

And she asked the nurse, "He's a boy?" And she said, "Oh, my God, how come? Why?" And she started crying, "Not a girl? I really had a hard time choosing to take on this pregnancy, and God did not give me a beautiful girl."

But, the nurse also said, "Don't worry. The next one is a girl."

And she said, "No, no, no way. I'm not going through another pregnancy, because I would never be sure. I would never know if it's a girl."

But, doctor said, "No, you're pregnant with twins, and pretty soon you're going to deliver a second child."

Then my mother delivered my sister one hour later. She said, "What is this child? Boy or a girl? I hope a girl."

The nurse and doctor were so happy, and said, "Yes, she's a girl."

My mother said, "Okay." Immediately, she said, "Does anybody want this boy? I don't mind if someone wanted to adopt him?"

A nurse said, "Oh, I want it. I want it. I'm going to take care of him," because this female nurse was not married and probably was happier to get a child that way.

But, my father did not let her adopt me.

Because I was born at seven and a half months and at a low weight — two pounds, two ounces — I had to stay in a hospital before I was safe to take home.

My mother took us home and finally had to hire somebody next door who had eight kids. One of the girls came over and took care of my sister. And that actually happened to my sister and my mother too, because she now had six kids; four of the kids were my father and mother's, and two were from his previous marriage, with six children total.

Also, our neighbor always had to work on a farm and put on dinner and lunch on the table. So, she came, and my father and mother decided it would be better to hire her. I'm sure it was just next door, but she mostly stayed with my parents. My father had a very big ranch, so he had plenty of room for her. Mostly, she stayed over there.

Everything was okay and in order. I was around seven years old when I found out my mother liked my sister in a different way. But it was okay; I was a child and not judging my mother or what was going on. When I went there and wanted to hug or kiss my mom, she didn't like to do that, but she did like to do that for my daughter, or she would give a hug to my daughter or her daughter.

But it was okay. I didn't think I had a chance to say very much. But my father was forty-seven years old when I was born and wasn't a person to enjoy giving hugs and kisses to kids. Mostly, he was busy with his own life and did not really care about kids very much. But again, I was not judging my father or mother. I was raised by them, and I had to accept what I got. Because I have no chance for complication because I would just be stepping on a problem or a punishment. So, I was used to what had happened.

My mother always watched me over her shoulder while I was busy doing something. But I always did my best to clean, sweep the floor, and make everything nice and in order to prove to my parents how good I was, how much I loved them, and how much I would do without saying anything. I didn't need a punishment and yelling to do something or not.

When I was about seven years old, my parents always had a rabbit, but somebody gave a rabbit to me. I made a mistake and tried to do it my own way. This was my own rabbit and I made a loose separate place, and it was at the same time I got two pairs of pigeons called "King Pigeon" — white, white, pure white King Pigeon — two pair. Then I tried to tell my parents or my mother, "Okay, this is mine. This is my pigeon."

My mother said, "No, you can't have it. There's no way somebody in this family can have their own business or say 'this is mine.'"

So, I said, "Okay."

This rabbit was female. The person who gave me the rabbit came over and brought his male rabbit to impregnate my rabbit. I never forgot the first time I had eleven small rabbits, and a pigeon made it so nice. My parents had a pigeon too, but not a King Pigeon, and it was a barn pigeon. I had a much smaller pigeon to butcher and then eat them. This King Pigeon had at least two pounds before it started to fly.

My family was so happy and then started to be interested. My mother said, "Okay, why not just buy more pigeons, at least King, and raise and sell them at a farmer's market?"

The same thing, so I built a bigger, well insulated pigeon coop. Under the attic, I put insulation in the rafters to make a better, warmer attic, and that way we had pigeons even in winter time. A small pigeon because sometimes in wintertime it went below zero, but this way it made it a much warmer building.

I also built a rabbit house. I made an underground rabbit house so in the summertime it would be nice and cool. Then I made the frame so the mosquitos would not bite the rabbit. I did not want the rabbit to get some terrible disease on its ears and nose. So, I did pretty well, but, of course, it was no way to corral my rabbit or pigeon. I did not tie it down. This man gave it to me. Actually, he gave me that rabbit. And after he gave me a male rabbit, black and white in color, I had many lists here I have this rabbit.

Of course, the more I petted these two rabbits the closer they got to me. But, of course, I had at least a couple hundred rabbits. Then finally I had at least a hundred King Pigeons I raised — a lot of small pigeons to sell in a flea market. I learned to butcher them, so I did butcher the rabbits, butcher the pigeons, and took them to a farmer's market. They even had a waiting list. I went with my parents to the farmer's market and people were waiting for us to drive into a farmer's market to pick up an order. I did pretty well.

Then, of course, my mother had not changed. Her mind was always mean to me. A nurse that took care of me in the hospital offered immediately to adopt me. She came once in a while to my parents' farm and gave me candy, which was bad since my mom got very upset and said her kids were not allowed to eat candy. So, I just accepted that I would not get it and she would not be able to give it to me. But the next time she came, she hid that candy for me. But, believe it or not, I was embarrassed and so sad I was unable to give candy to my other brothers and sister to share what I got. Because, if my mother to find out the nurse brought me candy, I would have gotten punished.

Time went by, and I always worked hard to please my parents. My mom chose my youngest brother as her the favorite son, and he did anything he wanted in the family, but I couldn't change that very much. It was only one thing; I had to accept it.

I finished elementary school. Of course, my parents weren't interested in sending me to school because I had enough talent to feed the cows, a horse, and sometimes I fed over twenty hogs my father owned. But mostly, I just gave the hogs water. I always worked, even though I was a kid. But I was so happy to do that again, buy love for my parents. I mean, it did not come true or ever happened.

But, of course, it's made in a pigeon and a rabbit on a farmer's market. They were happy to take the money I got for them. And, honestly, my two brothers and sister never gave a bit of help to me to raise rabbits or hogs. In the summertime, I cut the grass because rabbits liked to eat the grass very much. Also, I cut off branches from a tree because the rabbits liked to eat the leaves and small branches. I always made the entire farm so happy.

I always made the two cows and one horse so happy. Every morning I went in the barn and they would say hi to me with their own voices. A cow, a horse, and even the hogs were so happy to see me every morning. This is what made me them special in my heart; s that these animals gave me attention and love because I never knew what it meant to receive love, especially from my parents.

But it was okay. No one was the same. I wasn't saying they were bad parents. I had to be accepting and know I was not able to change anything when it came to that. But, at this time, I wouldn't go into too many details.

I went to a store for my parents, and then I would sweep the yard and shovel the snow in the wintertime. By the time I finished shoveling 100 to 200 feet of snow, I would take a look back and the wind would almost cover it again. I would not see what I had done since I started. But I really didn't have a choice but to just start over. I would not come back to do something else.

So, I finished my eighth year in elementary school. My father had one friend. I think he met him when he was in the army, and I think also my paternal grandpa knew him. So, he became a close friend and had an auto repair shop. He always knew me, and his wife always liked me. Actually, if I wanted love and hugs, he and his wife always gave them.

I also had an uncle, my father's brother, and he always liked me very much. He had a very nice wife and she always liked me when we got together. I saw her every day on our way to our school when I brought our three-liter milk. I'd dump the milk in on our way to school and picked it up on our way home. I always got candy or a little cookie from her, and she would give me a hug and kiss.

My uncle came to help my father, his brother, to do something else with construction. I also learned a lot about butchering from him. He did not teach me to butcher a rabbit or pigeon. I learned that from my mother. But he came when it was time to butcher the hogs. He came over all the time and I watched how he did it and I helped him.

I would come to his house all the time. He would butcher the hogs. The family would always come together to help each other. He knew how hard I worked and that I was separated from the other kids in the family when it came to love. Even in the family, I didn't have love. But God helped me get some attention from another person.

This man had an auto repair shop. I should mention his name was Steve. He often told my father, "This young boy finished school. But will he go into some kind of advanced school?"

My father said, "No, no, no. He has to stay on the farm."

Steve said, "Can I use him in my shop?"

My father said, "Well, I need to think about that, and I'll let you know."

I had farmer's market on Wednesday and Saturday, not too far from Steve's shop. So, my father and mother went to the next farmer's market. They delivered a product they were trying to sell at the farmer's market. He stopped over there to see Steve and said, "It's okay to use this boy, but you have to pay him. I'll let him work at your shop eight hours a day."

Then they made the deal. Steve was so nice, but he didn't have a child. He did not really make a big deal about cleaning the shop. It was okay, but I was not interested. So, the first week I cleaned everything and made it nice by organizing to be sure he could find everything. I just made him and his wife so happy.

Next door to his shop, he had a big house. He made one room for me. He said, "Ferenc, this is your room." He really accepted me like his own child or an adopted child. And then he said, "You know what, Ferenc? I'm doing something. Please don't tell anybody; just you, and me, and my wife. I will let you go to school today, and then you'll leave it all, the books and everything, in my house and not go directly to your parents."

I said, "Okay."

He said, "Any expenses that come up, I'm going to pay them."

So, he made it happen. I went to a school, an auto repair school, twice a week. Then, of course, before I went to work on his place, I had to feed the two cows and horse, warm the water for the hogs, and couple other chores before I left my house. At that point, because it was too far to walk to his place, Steve's brother gave me an old bicycle. Hoffman was the name and it was a German bicycle. Its name was a hard one. It was a very valuable bicycle. But both had a problem, so out of two bicycles I made one. I was so happy. I couldn't believe it. I was just walking. I rode the bicycle and couldn't believe how fast I made it to his place or the store. Before, I just walked to a store and held a big briefcase or baggage, without a bicycle, so everything just went very well. Steve and his wife took care of me like their own child.

The time came and I finished my studies after four years of school. My father went to the farmer's market and Steve had a friend, who was also a friend of my father's. His name was Joseph and his son went to the same school as me. Joseph knew my father very well.

He said, "Congratulations. My son told me your son has high grades when he finished school and what a nice student he is."

My father said, "What are you talking about? My son is not going to a school."

Joseph said, "I don't know. But you have a son. His name is Ferenc. He told me he's now finished with school."

My father went and talked to Steve. "What is Joseph talking about? What does this mean? What are you guys hiding here?"

Steve said, "Well, anyway he finished. You can't stop what I did for this boy. But he did finish auto repair school."

My father said, "Well, okay. He's now an auto mechanic. You need to pay more for him."

My uncle said it would be ten forint an hour, but he paid out fifteen or twenty because he paid for my school and food, and then he bought me a shirt and everything. He always gave it to my father because my father and mother did not let me keep the money. I always gave it to them. So, I did not see one dime. But I didn't need it. I didn't need to buy gas for a car. I had a bicycle. I had food in my house. My parents, so I eat. At Steve's house, I ate anything I wanted. I never really got new shirts or pants because I used my two brothers', and what they didn't use anymore. But it was okay. I was used to it.

Steve said, "Oh, no problem."

My father said, "You need to double his wage." My father's name was Sandor.

Steve said, "You know, Sandor? If you were asking me three times more money, I could pay you three times more for your son's labor." But he was not really happy. I mean, he was not happy at all with how my parents took care of me and raised me. But he wasn't able to say anything.

I did everything all the time. I took care of the pigeons and rabbits by raising them, butchering them, and then taking them out. I did it after I was finished with Steve's auto repair shop. Many times, I butchered them late in the evening or early in the morning. On Wednesdays and Saturdays, I went to the farmer's market.

The day before, I butchered them, and my family did not own a refrigerator or electricity, so it had to be done the day before, and then I got paid to deliver them. I would wake up very early in morning – 1:30 or 2:00 – to butcher the pigeons. I would start in the evening and do it all the way until 2 or 3 o'clock in the morning, practically without sleep because they would go with a horse buggy to farmer's market. By horse buggy, it took at least one hour to get there and I needed to be there very early.

I did not mention a little bit. When I was seven or eight years old, my father had one very bad friend. I didn't know why he made a friendship with him. But even he forced me to help this man. He always, always gave me a hard time and beat me very bad. He lost his wallet and blamed me and some bad things. He wanted me to work on this house, a very, very dirty job. He had me clean the outhouse and barn where the hogs were in a cage. But I always did everything my parents wanted me to do.

9

I finished auto repair school and I was still working for Steve. I became a nineteen-year-old and I met my first girlfriend. I never had a girlfriend before until somebody had a wedding and II met her there. She was an only child. She was a beautiful girl. She had a long hair; she would almost sit on her hair when on a chair. Everything went so well.

Her parents had money, but, for some reason, she was not the type of person who went to special clubs, dancing or going to movies. Mostly, she would stay home. I had a chance but my parents did not let me go dancing ever, so both of us stayed home. Even though we were in different situations, we were the same. It was interesting. She lived close to my parents' house. We would see each other once in a while. Steve was so happy to know I met this lady; her name was Julie. With Julie, everything went so well.

A year after I met her, my sister turned twenty, and on September 12, 1970, she had a wedding. My girlfriend, Julie, wanted to make it that day, but her cousin in Yugoslavia had a wedding on the same day. She had to go one way, and I went the other. She went to Yugoslavia and I had to stay with my sister.

My parents had one friend. I had another friend who had two children and always came to my house, but we had some miscommunication. So, this friend came to my parents' house and they had a boy and a girl. I last saw his daughter and son close to ten years ago. My mother went to a farmer's market with this woman.

Finally, this lady's mother had a boutique selling combs and kids' toys. The combs were made of bones from cow horns and not plastic. My mother went there just to see. But she went to my...I called her my "future wife" or I mean, I don't know how to discuss that there. But one friend, I mean, he had two kids and his grandma has a boutique and store for selling kids' toys and corn. My mother went there and did not see the grandma over there. She asked his daughter, "Where is Anna? What has happened to her?"

"Oh, you don't know? She died about a half year ago."

"What has happened to grandma?"

"Oh, she had an appendix something. I don't know how to say it, but she got dizzy, and after ten days, she died."

She took it over and said, "How are your kids doing?"

She said, "Oh, well, everyone is doing okay. What has happened? And how is your son doing? How is his sister, Ilonka, doing? And how is Ferenc doing?"

My mother said, "Well, I'm doing very well. And everything is the same. Believe it or not, but Ilona's wedding is a week to ten days from now."

Because that happened actually on Wednesday, which was farmer's market day, so it was a week from that Sunday she would get married.

The woman said, "Well, before that, what has happened? You don't mind if my daughter and son go to your sister's wedding?"

I said, "Of course, I don't mind."

This friend's son and daughter came to my parents' farm the next Sunday. I met this girl and boy after about ten years, and she was a beautiful girl. His son was okay. His brother was already eighteen years old; I was close to twenty, and he was a year younger than me.

So, I made the deal. The next Saturday they both came to the wedding. Because Julie, my girlfriend, had to go to Yugoslavia to attend another wedding, and I didn't have another girlfriend. At my sister's wedding, I stayed with four pairs of boys and girls. I sat next to my sister's future husband and she sat next to my sister. She was still over there and I spent the time with her.

The next week, Julie came back from Yugoslavia. Of course, she found out what had happened. By the next week, I saw her, and she was not nice to me.

She said, "Oh, I heard you already have a girlfriend."

I said, "She's not my girlfriend. It was just my sister. She wanted somebody to be with me since I was a groomsman."

It was interesting this girl came. I had not seen her in ten years. It looked like she liked me. I couldn't say I liked her. She was a beautiful girl, but I didn't have an idea of changing friendship with her and quit being with Julie because Julie was a beautiful girl to me.

Julie got upset and gave a ring back to me, but actually not at this time. She and her mother came to Steve's shop and weren't too nice to me. "Bring back a ring. Give it to me."

Steve told Julie and her mother this was a big mistake to give back the ring.

The next week on Tuesday, Marta, my old friend's daughter, she came to the shop because she was going to the hairstyling school that was next to Steve's shop. It was on the same road, but a meter and mile or half a mile.

She came over and said, "How are you doing?"

I said, "Fine. I am okay." Actually, earlier she asked me if I had a girlfriend. I said, "Yes, I have a girlfriend. But you asked me at the wedding if I had a girlfriend, and I said yes. But I need to tell you now I don't have a girlfriend. She quit. She found out you and I were together at the wedding. She's pissed off and does not want to continue that friendship."

So, that was in September.

Chapter 2
Marriage

After she asked me if I had a girlfriend or not, she stopped over on Tuesday. I explained to her everything that had happened. After she found out, she felt I was a person to have a friendship with and then, more and more, she would often stop over there in the shop.

I found out she had a very difficult time at home. She had a brother, and he was treating her very badly. Her parents were divorced and her father was living in a different city about six or seven-hour drive to the city where she lived. Her mother favored her son. I wasn't sure this was the reason her brother was mean to her. One day she came over and I saw she had a black eye.

Then next I asked, "Explain what has happened."

Her brother beat her because she and I became close friends too fast.

Closer to Christmas, we decided it would be better to make plans to marry. This was because I had a very difficult life at home, and she had an unhappy life at home also. We felt this would stop the pain by sharing a home and getting away from what I had at home.

I told her to go to a particular store to buy a an engagement ring; not a wedding ring, but just a friendship ring for commitment to becoming closer friends and boyfriend/girlfriend. I went to the jewelry store along with Steve and his wife to look at the ring. I found a beautiful ring. I liked it, but it was too expensive.

But Steve and Etelka said, "Don't worry. If she likes it, we're going to buy it."

They knew I didn't have any money because any money I made at auto repair shop was given to my parents. So, I wasn't able to save money.

Marta went to the jewelry store and, it was hard to believe, but she picked up the exact ring I picked up. So, Etelka went to the store and bought the ring.

That was very close to Christmas. In Hungary, Christmas was two days on the 25th and 26th. On the 25th, Christmas Day, I asked my parents if it was okay if I brought Marta, my girlfriend, to lunch on Christmas Day. Lunch was at noon. My mother said it was okay. She didn't know what the plan was.

Marta came over and I told my parents the plan. I already had the ring in my pocket. So, I showed my parents the ring Steve and his wife bought. My mother and father got very upset by what I thought, and said, "No way." Even my mother wanted to take away the ring. She said I needed to take it back to Steve. She did not realize I called Steve.

What had happened was, this time, I did not fight with my parents. For the first time in my life, I said no. I held that ring strongly in my hand. I put my hand in my pocket and did not let them take it out.

Then my mother and my father said, "If you're not going to change your mind, then you have to move out of the house immediately."

I said, "What do you mean, immediately?"

she said, "Now."

I did not mention it earlier, but I had a motorcycle. It was a Gawa. Steve and his wife bought it for me when I turned eighteen years old. My parents were not interested in buying a motorcycle for me, but they bought a motorcycle for my youngest brother. My oldest brother had a motorcycle many years before.

My youngest brother said, "Motorcycles cost 18,000 forints."

My cousin, my favorite uncle's son, had an older motorcycle, a Gawa. He said, "I'm going to buy that one for 6,000 forints and keep the 12,000 forints for my future life."

At that time, my brother was not married yet.

I asked my parents, "Are you serious? I need to move out of the house if I do not change my mind?"

She said, "Of course I am. You don't have another option. Give me the ring and I'll take it back to Steve, or you need to get out of the house."

Well, I never had many pants and shirts and everything, just enough for daily use. At this time, I did not change my shirt every day, just once a week. So, I didn't have very much stuff. I picked up and put a couple away in one second.

Then my mother took over, looked at that, and said, "Well, it's okay. Take this one. But you can't take anything else."

So, I had my own pillow and blanket. I said, "Can I take my pillow and blanket?"

She said, "No. If you pay for it, you can take it. If not, it's not yours."

Of course, I didn't have any way to pay for it. My parents kept every penny of what I made.

So, then I tried to give a hug and kiss to my mom and hug for my father, and they did not let me do it. My heart was broken, and then God made it better. I just went on my own way. Then I took Marta home. I gave it to her then I took her home.

I went to Steve and explained everything. Steve and his wife were both crying and hugging me. They said, "We have been waiting a long time for this day."

I already had my own room in his house. Steve didn't have a child. He said, "Ferenc, I already told you, you can feel at home. This is your home and a peaceful home. Just don't worry about it."

Then my life was illuminated, and I had tears in my eyes. I thanked my uncle and aunt.

Even today, it's hard to explain that.

I went to school for three and a half years. Steve had been paying for that.

And then, you're not going to believe what happened. Marta came over, but not on Tuesday this time. She came over on a Monday and had a black eye and was crying. She said, "I don't think I'm able to go home because I tried to explain to my mom what happened. And then she was very mean to me."

So, I went over to my mother-in-law's place the next Saturday. We had lunch, I tried to explain what had happened, and why I'd like to get married. But, at that time, my fiancé was not working. She was still in a school. She went to a hairstyling school. I explained everything to her mom.

Of course, she said, "Get out of my house and stay away from my daughter. I don't want you to see her ever again."

I asked Marta, "What do you think? Would you like to come with me or stay here? Or would you like to continue our friendship and date more? Or would you like to take your mom's advice?"

She said, "No, no, no. I don't want to change my mind. I want to be married to you, and I want to stay with you like we are now, like a girlfriend/boyfriend."

We set a date to be married on April 24, 1971. Her mother said, "If you are not changing your mind, get out of my house," and then she pushed her; it was very sad. (I have this in my other book, but I'll say it now). My future mother-in-law spat on and kicked me, and said, "Get out of my house."

Marta was able to pick up a couple personal things. I said, "Don't worry. Steve and his wife will help you out one way or another." I drove to Steve's house and said, "Well, you let me stay at your house, but I have another problem. Marta, my fiancé, was kicked out."

Steve said, "Well, don't worry about it. I'm going to take care of this problem."

Etelka was a strong, religious person, and said, "I don't want you guys living in my house without being married."

Steve had a brother, and his brother had one daughter, but they lived in a big house. So, Steve called his brother. His brother had a telephone, too, because his brother had a business— a construction business. Not everybody had a telephone in Hungary at this time. He explained everything to him.

His wife said, "Don't worry. Just bring Marta over here now."

They were not too far from Steve's house. They brought Marta over and she lived in a room that was already set up because he had a big house and only one child who still lived there. The money I earned at Steve's place, he let me keep. I put the money together to pay the expensive wedding costs. I bought a black suit for me and a white suit for Marta and the engagement ring.

Steve offered to help me, but I said, "This time, I thank God you helped me by letting me stay at your house, and you have not charged me anything. I have been able to save a little bit of money and I'd like to spend that money."

He said, "This is very nice that you want to do it your own way. But if you are ever need more money, just let me know. I'm glad to help you." So, it was okay.

April 24, 1971: I got married in the same church I was baptized as a Catholic. It was a very nice church. I had the money to buy a suit and everything I needed for the wedding. But, really, I didn't have the money to have a big wedding; just Steve and his wife, his brother and his brother's wife and daughter came to my wedding. That was all I needed. So, everything went very well.

I did marry, then rented a tiny room where we could stay together. For a couple of weeks, we slept on the floor. But I did it to start my own life with my own money, even when Steve once again offered to give me more money and help out if I needed it. What happened was Steve's brother had an old, small ranch house and his brother offered to let me stay at this house; he had a garage and we went into this garage. Steve's brother had a small ranch house that his parents had before. But his mother and father had died, so it was empty, and didn't have electricity.

Marta and I decided to move into this very nice, small house. It was a cute, white, small ranch house. Then what happened was Marta finished hairstyling school in August; when we got married it was her last year. So, by the middle of August, she started working as a hairstylist.

I was working at Steve's place while attending electrician school. I had a special way to go to school in doing a test. Every course had to pick up homework once a month and go through a bit at school one day from 9:00 A.M. to 9:00 P.M. Actually, it was a long day during the course. Every course had a test. I chose to attend a two-year electrician school program. I had a chance to repair that oil burner. At that time, I started to sell automatic washing machines in Hungary. There were no dryers yet in Hungary, just washing machines. So, then I decided if I finished school, I had more of a chance to work and make money. So, I attended this school besides working for Steve.

I also started to pick up cars from friends and strangers and took them to this small house in the garage. I would change the engine or rebuild the transmission. Steve was happy to see that, and he even helped me. Steve was not a young person. I had a chance to get a nice, small auto repair shop, so I rented one in the city. But when I rented that small auto repair shop, it did not come out very well because it was too small and the city was not happy to work over there on a car. I continued to work for Steve.

Chapter 3
Farm in Hungary

Because the small auto repair shop did not work out, I continued to work in Steve's shop. I already had a built up a customer base, and he let me work on my customers' cars. Plus, I did well at electric school, too. At school, I got my electrician's license. I had a client for repairing oil burner appliances, and I did volunteer work on an automatic washing machine. So, I did pretty well. The major work I had already mentioned earlier. I finished it in a small ranch house garage.

My wife and I decided to have a child, and then my wife got pregnant. We drove to a city back and forth to see whether its condition was good for a motorcycle. If we could not make it with a motorcycle, we used the auto bus going back and forth to the city and then to our farmhouse.

When my wife was about six months pregnant, she met her mother in a grocery store; at that time, we didn't have a supermarket in Hungary. She saw she was pregnant and went over to talk to Marta. "Well, I hear you are doing very well, and I'm glad to see you're waiting for a baby." Then her mother said, "I hope you are not upset with me."

My wife said, "Of course, I'm not upset. I never was upset with you, but you did not let me stay in your house. I really love Ferenc, and Ferenc loves me, and he saved me. So, of course, I moved out."

She said, "I would like for you both to come to my house next weekend."

My wife said, "Well, I need to talk to Ferenc about that. But I think he wouldn't mind."

My mother-in-law came to my workplace. She was lucky I was there because sometimes I would go to somebody's house or pick up auto parts at a store, and then go to somebody's house to look at a car if it wouldn't start. Sometimes I went to the auto parts store because, in my country, they would not deliver the parts at this time. I would have to go to get them. Sometimes I would go to the capitol in Hungary, Budapest, to pick up parts so I would be gone all day. But, of course, that was when I did it about once or twice a month since it was so far. It would cost about a whole day to do it.

My mother-in-law met me over there and explained what was happening. She gave me a hug.

I said, "Thank you. Thank you. I am really, really glad to see and talk to you."

So, the next weekend we went to her house, and in the back, they had a large property. That house was his mother's house, or my wife's grandma's house originally, and the back had a shop.

She worked on manufacturing combs using bone and hairclips, and so many nice things were made in that shop. They did not use plastic, but bone to make the combs. But she died, and then the shop had been closed for a long time. My mother-in-law asked if I wanted to make this shop into living quarters. She was so happy to see that and didn't even mind spending money to buy what was needed — a new window, and there was no bathroom in this building — so really it was a complicated matter again.

I was lucky because I learned construction from my uncle. He came to my father's house doing construction and I always — beginning when I was just seven — wanted to learn to do something. Also, when he had a construction project in his house, I went there. Or, if the family had any construction project, my father would let me do it because a lot of friends and relatives of my father knew how well I did so many things. They always made a deal with my father to let me help even when I was so busy.

So, what had happened was I finished the building four days before my wife delivered my daughter. That happened on August 29, 1972. That was the second biggest day of my life. First of all, of course, when I married my wife it completely changed my life. Because I had missed my parents' hugs and love, even though my uncle and his wife were so nice to me. Steve and his wife gave me hugs and liked me all of the time. But, of course, everybody knew when you married somebody it made a difference. I didn't have to say how big a difference since people already believe it.

I had my daughter. She was just a beautiful girl and there were no complications. In my country, it was required for new moms to stay at the hospital for four days. I couldn't wait until the fifth day to bring her home. I would never forget when I gave her the first evening bath. Everything went so well.

My mother-in-law was so happy. The first week in the last four or five days, she came down and had tears in her eyes, and then said, "Thank you, God. Thank you, Ferenc. You did such a nice job on your marriage. You are so nice to my daughter and so nice to me. And you did a beautiful job on the building." She was just so happy.

Her son, my wife's brother, was in the army at that time. In the Hungarian Army, they required soldiers stay in a building. He came home every three or four months, or two or three time a year. So, finally, he came home and saw a big change in the building; he saw a beautiful child, and then apologized to me. He hugged me and said, "It's unbelievable how nice a job you did, Ferenc."

I said, "Not just thanks for me, thank you for your sister, too." And then everything went so well.

I was working at Steve's shop because he was sixty-seven years old, and slowly stopped working at the auto business and gave me all the customers. And then, of course, as I already mentioned, I had built up customers also. I made pretty good money, and then was able to handle it, financially, to have my wife stay home after she delivered my daughter. Not that I worked hard — I always worked hard — but now I was the only person to make money. But I handled it and was happy to see her stay home with my daughter.

In Hungary – and I think all over Europe, not just Hungary – everyone would have lunch at noon. Of course, it was a small breakfast, a huge meal at noon, and then in the evening a little snack. Sometimes, I would have a snack at 4:00 P.M. and then in evening another small snack, but nothing major. Also, when I would go home I would always like to take a half-hour nap. Many times, my sweet daughter would sleep next to me. She slept on my arm and was so happy, and then I would go back to work.

I earned money to buy a building. Steve found out somebody had a 123-year old building that needed major remodeling on a huge lot. It had an extra one-acre garden in the backyard. That house had a shop on the property, a basement, and an auto garage. The auto garage was actually called a carport. But I turned the carport into a garage after I bought. I fixed and lived in a small, cute ranch house.

Oh, okay, sorry. I missed something. I lived in my mother-in-law's house at this time, but I still had a small ranch house. It looked cute, so I kept it. Because it was so far, time-wise I had to step out of this small ranch house. I just spend the time to work on this big building and not going back and forth to do any auto repair where I needed business on a house. I gave it to back to Steve's brother.

During the day, I would be working on a car, and during the evening I would work on this building. Not always, but any time I had spare time I had to do remodeling. I did it. Also, when I had to work on some project, I would not substitute it out to a contractor. I just hired people looking to make a little extra money. I checked out how these people were doing on the job because I knew remodeling very well. As I mentioned already, I learned how it needed to be done. But, of course, I did some of it, and then I had to hire a helper to do it and check over to make sure the helper was doing a good job.

So, the house I bought over there – I'm sorry I did not mention it earlier – Steve helped me buy it. I had already earned some money to put down 50% on that project. Steve helped me with some money to do it. I had two years to pay another 50%. So, that way I was able to work on the remodeling of the building. Of course, Steve watched over me again to make sure I had enough money to finance this project.

He even said, "I not going to ask you. Here is some money, whether you need it or not. Take it and just work on this building and finish this."

I was so happy. I was busy and everything was just so nice.

My wife and I decided to have another child, and then the kids would grow up together. Later it would be much better in the future, as they wouldn't have a big age difference between them. So, we made it happen. My wife delivered a second baby, a boy, on February 24, 1975. Again, she did so well, and it was extremely nice. There were no complications during the pregnancy or delivery.

Of course, as I mentioned earlier, she was in the hospital for four days. On the fifth day, I brought her home. I couldn't say how happy my daughter was to see her newborn baby brother. And my wife, of course, was content to stay home with the two babies. At that time, I bought a new washing machine and changed out the old-fashioned washing machine. We didn't need to do it by hand with a crank to wash the clothes. I bought an electric automatic washing machine. At that time – I already mentioned it previously – these washing machines just came out first in Hungary. In Europe, there were no dryers, just a machine that took the washed clothes and spit them out to get out of the water but no dryer. So, she was so happy.

My mother-in-law liked her two grandbabies. It was very interesting. Many times, one way or another way, I would see my parents and would wave and say hi all the time. But, in the beginning, though, my parents would not accept my wave. Then, I saw it one time. My mother waved and said hi back to me.

My father and mother were together at the same time I was at a hardware store.

I thought, *Okay, I'm going over there to say hi.* Then I gave a hug to my father and mother, and they let me do it.

My mother said, "I heard you guys are doing pretty well."

I said, "Well, I think so, too."

A couple weeks later, I saw my parents. They said, "Well, let's forget what happened before. If you want to come to my house, bring the grandkids and you can come here, too."

I said, "Okay." So, I did.

The house remodeling came out very well. I did it in one year. After I bought it, in about ten months, the house was finished. I decided not to keep the house but sell it because I found a condominium. It had two and a half bedrooms and two bathrooms with a two-car garage — a new condominium. I decided to buy it to move out of my mother-in-law's place.

I found a new building. It was a beautiful place. There was a person waiting for me to finish construction on a big house, in order to buy it; waiting for me to say, "Yes, it's for sale," and then let him know the price. Finally, the house was finished. I sold it at an extremely high profit margin. I had plenty of money to give back to Steve. I had plenty of money to pay the condominium off in full, and I still have money left over to do something. Besides, I would work extremely hard at the auto repair shop and electric repair, that included appliances and repairing some TVs, too.

I had already contacted my parents. My grandpa had eighteen sisters and brothers. But my father's family was extremely wealthy. My grandpa had hundreds of acres of land. My father made an offer to me. He said, "Ferenc, if you want some land, I don't mind giving you what you want."

I know there was a building built in 1864 next to my grandpa's old house. It was a beautiful old ranch house. It was also huge because there were eighteen kids that lived in this house. A big one, as it probably had 15,000-20,000 square feet altogether.

I said, "Well, it has three acres. I'd like to have it." But the three acres were a worthless piece of land. There was nothing on the land for many years, just grass.

My father said, "I have many pieces of land with good soil. Why do you want these three acres? They're worthless."

I said, "Well, I don't have a plan to go into an agriculture business. Maybe I will do something on that piece of land. But I don't know. I really just like these three acres."

About a week later, my father said, "Okay, I'll let you come and do the paperwork."

So, I got these three acres of agricultural land and then this happened: around the end of September, I got my name on this piece of land. All winter I thought about having land also. This was owned by my grandpa. My great grandpa actually bought this land around the 1820s. So, the land had been in my family's name for many, many years. You would not believe it. This land was just like sand. You would look at it and think it was worthless or very good for grapes or an apple orchard probably. Somebody probably even about doing that.

So, I decided to build a greenhouse the following spring. I built a big greenhouse, a huge one. I cut off branches and made the frame for that. Then

I put plastic on the greenhouse. I put a lot of manure — from horses, cows, and hogs — on the soil. I made my own well. At that time, we didn't have access to electricity. But I bought a huge generator and that was interesting. The generator came from United States. The name of this generator was "Mia"; it was a very, very old diesel engine. The well was built together with a generator, and then I also used the same engine, a Mia, with a water pump where you pumped the water from the well. Either way, I was able to pump the water with the diesel engine or use the generator to make power to use the electric motor to pick up the water. It was not a very big deal to make the well on that property because the water was only about twenty-five feet. I would go down to about twenty-five feet and had the water table was very good.

I did pretty well with the greenhouse. Everybody just watched it. "Oh, look at Ferenc. He has this worthless land and he's making a fortune on that piece of land."

I grew tomatoes and paprika. It grew much earlier compared to what came out from outside without a greenhouse. I brought the premier plus to a market about at least two or three months earlier because I did it in a greenhouse. I doubled the plastic on the greenhouse. A double layer made it warmer so everything worked well.

Because I liked it so much, even as a seven-year-old, I started feeding cows and a horse. When I was eight and a half years old, I started milking the cows. I found out it was not possible to get a special tax break from having a dairy farm. But even though I had this idea, it was very costly, financially. So, I said, "Well, I'm not ready to do that. But I'm able to build a building. I have money to build a building for raising geese."

I bought material to build a building to raise geese. Geese season was about six or seven months, and after that I didn't want the building to stay empty. I got about 4000-5000 geese every month. When geese season was over, I started to raise chickens. I always had a new generation of small chickens every six week.

The business worked out very well, so I earned enough money to step into a dairy business. I built a barn to raise fifty heads of dairy cows. I had these three acres, but I didn't have enough space to make a big pasture for that dairy farm. In my country, the cows did not really stay outside of a building. It was with chain tied to their necks and they stay inside a barn.

I built this barn. I did the construction, but in an interesting way. I would never forget that one. I used 272 posts and had rafters. On the side of the building, I used a green cane, but before I put that on, I welded the rafters on the rafter frame. I used again cane fourteen solution, that way nothing could break. Just a post and a cane sidewall about one foot wide, and then the top roof I made about another foot. I made the special brace holding a cane up next to the rafters, that way building in the summertime made it extremely nice and cold, and in the wintertime, amazingly nice and warm. Of course, I had fifty dairy cows and no problem for a heater. So it was not cold in the building.

So, of course, I did not do everything. I hired people. I got to the point where people were working for me in auto repair shop. I hired people and taught them by overlooking how they were working on the electric repair business. Of course, I did the same thing in auto repair. I had people help feed the geese and putt new straw in a barn, morning and evening, to keep it clean in the barn.

Then the time came to deliver the geese. I always hired people to help me put them in a car— chicken and the geese. I found people to work on the dairy farm. But, for some reason, I liked to do it. I always woke up at 3 o'clock in the morning to milk twenty-five cows. I liked to do that. It was in my blood.

I couldn't say my wife was too happy to see that. I woke up pretty early, but she was used to it.

She said, "It's okay. You like to do that? It's okay, then," because my hands were tied doing so many things.

Even when I watched how my employees were doing, it was a lot of time and work. But I was always raised to work hard, so it was nothing new to me.

So, I had everything working so well. But my mother let me go into the ranch house. But because she had very bad memories about rich people or somebody who had money, it didn't matter how nice I was to her. I brought her and my father their favorite food.

I have to mention: My older brother was working for the government for small wages. I knew he wanted to build his own house.

I always liked to do something in the city where they were building a new shopping center and had an old building. They wanted to tear down many of these buildings. I had in my mind to build another little building on my farm. In Hungary, it was always hard to get lumber and extremely expensive. So, in the beginning, I decided, I would go to an auction and buy the house, and then I would hire somebody to tear down the building.

I went to this place that had plans to tear down many buildings to build a new shopping center. I found a small building, and it had very good roof material and everything else was extremely good. But a lot of people were bidding on that building and I got to the point it was not worth buying.

Then the last building was a huge building. It was more than 200 years old. Nobody wanted to buy it because everybody was afraid to buy it. It was extremely big. I started the bidding by raising my hand, and then they said, "One, two, three."

Chapter 4

United States

I had this dairy farm and everything. I bought this building, and then I hired people to tear it down. It had many great materials in this building. I helped my brother and sister to build a house. My older brother built it on his wife's parent's land. My youngest brother had a lot, but his wife's parents gave it to them. My twin sister had the same thing – a lot in the city – but her husband's parents gave it to them.

I was a person who always liked to give something, but I did extremely well with the farm and the geese and the chickens. With the auto repair shops, I made pretty good money. Then I got to help my sister's brother. I got all the bricks and roof material needed for a building. I was even able to help a little bit financially to do it.

I had this big farm, not because I was money hungry or needed more money. I just did it to do it. My father always said I was identical to his father, or my grandpa. He had a lot of property. I did not want to create it to do badly. I did pretty well and didn't mind having more.

I finished tearing down this big building and made great money on that building also. I started over there to mention was my oldest brother worked in the government and then I built a building to let him work over there. He got over 2000-2500 geese every four weeks, and with the season over, about 24,000 chickens.

I helped him do it financially. He really did not need to spend one dime to step into this business. He needed to work over there. In the morning he worked about two or three hours, and in the evening two or three hours, and he earned about ten times more money; he made more money in one month than he did working for the government for a whole year. I didn't think anyone knew that. But he actually made double the money in one month what he made in a whole year exactly because I knew how small his wages were in the government.

Besides that, I did very well. But I stepped into a problem. What started to happen was what I called "the jealous people" saw I was doing very well more and more and people thought:

"Ferenc, he has more and more money."

What was even more sad was my mom saw my projects were quickly growing bigger.

I started a dream of constructing another building and stepping toward another project to build a place to raise hogs. I wanted to buy a hundred mother hogs and raise about 700 to 1000 hogs. Each season needed about seven to eight months to take them to a place for slaughter. This really made my mother change her attitude.

As I mentioned earlier, I helped my oldest brother. My sister also came over and delivered the geese. She helped a little bit, but she was never a hard worker or ever interested. But she was interested to the point where she could get a little more money, and then I was happy to give it to her. Because, again, I made much more money.

I helped, not only my sister and brother, but many other people buy something. At this time in Hungary, a person had to put down a 50% down payment for a car, or to buy a co-op and needed to claim some money, one had to wait a couple years to get it.

Some people came to me and said, "Can I borrow money to buy that and that?"

I said, "You know what? I like you and I have known you for many years. You haven't been rude to me and I want to keep it that way. Please, come and work on my farm, and I will pay you very well. And then you'll have money for a down payment."

Because my farm quickly grew, I had in my mind to complete another project. I had a black Holstein and wanted to buy another red Holstein to make it 100 head dairy farms. I couldn't make the geese farm bigger because of the extremely high tax rate. On a dairy farm – in my country, in Hungary at that time – it was tax-free and hogs too. So, I did very well and I even had to stop milking fifty head cows because, at that time, I couldn't handle it anymore. I just needed to check over everything to make sure it was going well because it was a big project and time concern.

Very sad – so then my youngest brother and sister, I helped her. She worked by doing something or not, but I knew she needed help. My oldest brother had a chance to raise chickens and geese. My youngest brother had treated me totally different all the time, but I did not want him to come over to do daily work. He was just interested in cleaning the barn and take out all the manure for the week from the geese or six weeks from the chickens. Somebody cleaned the dairy farm, but in the next building. My youngest brother took the cow manure, but I gave it to him for free and he sold it for a lot of money.

My mother and brother went their jobs. But it was my mother who handled this thing to see if I had more money. I didn't know how she did not see it because I was on the way to my farm and my car headlight was pointed to her window past her bedroom. She thought my life was really worthless because I only wanted to spend the time with my kids or family. She thought I had to be working 365 days a year. I woke up every single morning at 3 o'clock. But, I did not think about it that way. I wanted to do the work, and I was happy to do it.

I started building a hogs' farm building.

My mother said, "Ferenc, are you going to construct another building, or start on a new thing next my house?"

Actually, this was not her house. That was my grandpa's house. He built it on my great grandpa's land in 1864. There was already some building over there. He really made the building enormous in 1890 but had some building in 1864. It was made because my grandpa had eighteen kids and finished construction around 1912. There was always more space needed, since he had more kids. Then he had more things on his mind, like I did it. I was growing bigger and bigger.

I didn't know how serious my mother was with what she said. So, I started construction for the hog farm, an automatic feeder, and everything came to the shop, a piece of land next to the barn. This happened about Monday afternoon. I had a little building on the farm, but I used one room upstairs while visiting my grandpa's house or my father's house. I didn't know how I would say that.

I had to go inside my parent's ranch; it had one gate. I saw that the gate was locked with a big chain. I just couldn't believe what had happened. The gate was locked and my mom saw that I walked over and I wanted to go inside the ranch house.

She said, "No, no, no way. You can't come in my house anymore because I said so. You're doing more construction here. I don't want to talk to you anymore. You are not allowed to come out to my place."

I did not tell her, "This is not your place. This is my father's place." That building came from my grandpa, and the land from my great grandpa, so it had been in the family for many, many years. But it was okay. I did not say anything. I didn't want to hurt my mom.

It was interesting. This had a gate here. But if I went around a building, since it was a farm, there was no gate or anything in back of the ranch. I said, "Mom, you know I want to go inside the house. I'm going around the building so I can do what I want to do. But I'm not going to do it unless you take this chain off, please. Don't lock me out of your heart because I am very happy to return to everything being normal and loving each other." I said, "You saw I have a nice farm. I have a nice marriage with kids, and everything is going very well." And then I said, "You know my happiness is my wife staying home with my kids. I am working very hard to do it."

The only way I could spend time with my daughter was to have her come to the farm. As I already mentioned, my wife did not really want my son to come to the farm, but he was not interested either. But my daughter did.

I did not take what my mother did seriously. But the next morning, I had some stuff in my parents' house. I went to my farm and the sun had just come up. I saw my personal stuff and some other vegetables and so many things I had inside the farm because it had room. My mother had thrown out everything by the fence and still had not taken off the chain.

I said, "Well, what can I do? I'm unable to do anything and can't change her mind."

After that day, youngest brother agreed to take manure to my place. But that did not mean he did not want it. Really, he was doing me a favor because I signed up for other people for pretty good money. My oldest brother agreed to work over there.

I said, "Well, you think you're that dumb. It's okay. Go ahead and do it." Hundreds of people wanted to come over to do the same as what he did.

Immediately, I found relatives to take over the project for my older brother. and then other people came and were so happy to just take the manure. I continued construction on the hogs building and also built a small bedroom, a little living room, and then a bathroom. Not bad. There was one room in the kitchen and everything was about 25 feet by 25 feet. There was one room made into a bathroom to take a shower if anybody wanted.

Continuing through this sad story: My mother and youngest brother made things more difficult for me.

I needed to put that in this story. Yes, in my country, there was strong communism. But, really, it was somebody paying a tax and I paid a lot of taxes to the government. For example, I made about seven million forint a year and paid about 85% on taxes and health insurance. They took about 85% away. But that is a lot of money.

I built this building on a property that was worthless, three acres, because, for at least twenty to forty years, it was used for nothing since nobody knew what to do on this piece of property. I thought my grandpa or great grandpa had grapes on that property years ago. My father, for some reason, did not continue with their work, instead choosing to build on these three acres. Not just these three acres, but the twenty acres sitting next door were doing nothing and wild grass grew on it.

In 1983, around February or March – I didn't know exactly what time, but around March, I left the farm. I went home to take a shower and eat and spend time with my children and wife. I told my wife I had a bad feeling. I had to return to the farm. So, I went back at 9:30 to 10:00 P.M. About a mile before the farm, I saw its flame. It was going up and down. One section had all the medicine for the cows and chickens and many expensive things. Because my parents kicked me out of the big farmhouse I first did a small section. I split it to keep the equipment and everything out we needed for the farm. For this reason, I wanted to make it a nicer place to start building another construction project and make a cleaning room; I built a room for my employees, a shower, a little storage, a place for me to have lunch plus clean dairy equipment, and five-pound buckets that held the milk.

My neighbor said – I never say that even all the way up to today – my youngest brother did it but somebody said it. Over there the next-door neighbor said to me my youngest brother went on the farm. Whether he did or not, I didn't want to know.

My youngest brother so it had happened before. After that, a county officer came over. He said, "Well, Ferenc, you built this building without permit. And this is agriculture land."

I said, "Why should I call this agriculture land? Look at it. It's doing nothing on this piece of land here." I had to pay a very high tax, and then I helped a lot of people to earn money.

He said, "It doesn't matter. You do not have a permit. You did it."

But, of course, this man was a very strong communist. My youngest brother and mother held a tape measurer to help him measure the building to penalize me.

That story is very hard for me because it still hurts me very bad.

I only had a little section burned where somebody started the fire. Even the fire department – this was my building, not the government's building – penalized me a lot of money because I had a fire on my ranch.

The county measured the building size and gave me an extremely high penalty for building it. The penalty was 10 million forints.

In 1983, 10 million forints was a lot of money. How should I explain it? A government job would make about 50,000 forint a year. Definitely good, but mostly 25,000-30,000 forints, but some made pretty good money; 50,000 forint a year. I was penalized a 10 million forint.

I paid a very high penalty, but still made close to 1.2 million forint a month, which is about 10-15 million a year. So, I made a profit. But, again, not because I needed it for me. I helped a lot of people who needed it. It got to a point where it was more serious with more jealous people, and they were watching what I was doing over there. But when anybody did anything for me, I would close my eyes and not say anything. I almost said, "Well, too bad because you're doing that to me. I am still okay, so everything going very well, so no problem."

But what my mother and youngest brother did to me, I couldn't handle it. I talked to my lawyer to find out what was the best thing to do.

He said, "Well, Ferenc, I don't think these people will leave you alone. You need to think about taking steps to move to a different county in Hungary. A lot of people immigrate to stay away from this communism. You go ahead and consider which is the better option for you."

My story – I mentioned it already – in 1975, I visited the United States to see another relative. My daughter and son had a hard time because of communism in school and this hurt me very bad. I don't know. Communism had always stayed in this country because Russia was closer to Hungary. It had been around about ninety years. I did not say anything. Poland and East Germany, communism was just terrible. Nobody knew whether it was getting worse or if it would someday quit.

I decided to move to the United States. I worked very hard to get passports for the whole family because a lot of people got passports for a father and one child, or a mother and one child. But under communism, if somebody had money, you did anything you could to get a permit, or getting t a permit through the government.

But again, what was hurting me very bad was that my mother and brother went against me, and I couldn't handle it. This was one thing. Another thing was my children had a hard time in the school. I knew I had a very smart daughter, and my son was very smart, too. But he studied much harder, unlike my daughter. That was the difference. You know, that is not an unusual thing what I said. Some people just read something once and memorize it immediately. Another one could read it ten times and have a very hard time memorizing it.

I hired my lawyer. He helped me get the whole family passports. That way I was able to step over the border on August 17, 1983. I immigrated to the

United States. In August of 1983, I went to Austria and waited there for the paperwork to make sure I was cleared of everything, and to see if the FBI or Interpol was not looking for me because I had a very strong political reason to start a new life.

I did have a chance to go to the United States pretty fast. I stepped on U.S. soil with my family on December 19, 1983. I started in New York. I had a relative, my nephew, who lived in New York in 1983. I arrived at the John F. Kennedy Airport in the afternoon about 4 o'clock. It was interesting. My nephew, at 8:00 P.M. on this day, left the United States to go to Hungary. I met him over there for a couple of hours before he left.

My niece also lived in New York City — Astoria, New York. She took me home to her brother's house. It was interesting at her brother's house. He was single at that time. He had a very nice apartment in a nice building, but it had cockroaches all over. At this time, one winter was stronger, one winter was mild. Anyway, it was all over the place, this difference in weather. But the biggest problem his apartment had was the cockroaches and I was unable fix that. I tried to plug the hole to stop them from coming inside the building. My daughter had never seen a cockroach before and was afraid to go to the bathroom. My son and I brought my dog to the United States and he was scared on the street because he never had known this kind of big population in a city.

My wife had a relative in California, so she contacted them. I even got a ride to the United States on December 19th. In the morning on the 21st, I got Social Security on Broadway in Manhattan at the Social Security office. On the 22nd at 2 o'clock in the afternoon, I started working at a shop in New York – a Hungarian from Romania. He used to be Hungarian and he spoke my language.

Do you know how I found him? I asked my niece about finding a job, but she was not an expert, especially since I didn't speak any English.

One thing I said, "Okay, I'm going to pick up a telephone book." The telephone book I think had 3400 pages. I was looking for a Hungarian in the business section. I knew that auto repair places were called "auto repair".

I found one person who had a Hungarian name. I called him and then he said:

"Well, it's on a holiday. My business is not open. But if you want it, I can give you a man's name. He's working up the street and he's the youngest. He's Romanian/Hungarian who speaks your language, and he might hire you."

I called his number. He said, "Come to my place tomorrow. I'm busy in the morning, but I'd like to see you at 2:00 P.M."

So, I went. He told me how to go on the subway. That subway, not a subway, not a subway. Just in case, I left at 11:30 or before 11 o'clock — not 11:00, 10:20, closer to 11:00 — to be sure I was able to make it over there on time. I didn't want to be late to the appointment. I asked God to help me have the chance to get there about 1:15, 1:30. Way before 2:00.

I said, "I'm sorry I came earlier, but I just wanted to make sure I would not miss this appointment." I introduced myself and explained what my story was.

He said, "Do you want to work after the holiday?"

I said, "No, no, no. I don't have very much money, and I have two children. I'd like to work as soon as possible."

He said, "What is as soon as possible?"

I said, "If you have things to do, I don't mind working now."

He said, "Are you serious? Are you kidding me? But your shirt and hands are going to get too dirty."

I said, "I don't care. But the money you are going to give me, that one is clean."

He said, "Wow. Looks like you're different from many other people." He even suggested I go to the immigrant office and get a check to start to live on.

I said, "No, no, no. I'm okay. I would just like to start work now."

So, what happened was he gave it to me. He said, "Well, I'm going to give you about $4 an hour."

I said, "Okay."

I worked there until he closed the shop around 7:00 P.M. He said, "Well, I start tomorrow morning around at 8:00."

I said, "Well, I hope I make it home now. I made it here, but I need to figure out how I make it home." I told my family, especially my wife, I was so happy I got the job.

I left the next morning at 5 o'clock to be sure I made it over there. I liked it even better. On another day, I was there way before 8:00, and then I worked all day.

Before Christmas, I had one more day to work for them and he said, "Well, I told you it would be $4 an hour. But you have children and you did an amazing job here. It's been a while, but somebody said that this auto mechanic knows what he's doing." He paid me immediately $6 an hour, so I had a very nice Christmas.

I had some money, but still didn't have much: no warm clothes because I left Hungary in August. I had to go down to buy some stuff. I went to one store in Astoria, and then looked for food. It was very interesting. It had special food for Christmas Eve made with poppy seed and a small piece of bread. I was looking for poppy seed.

One lady there was watching me and my family, and said, "Oh, oh, you're Hungarian?"

I said, "Yes, we are Hungarian."

She said, "How long have you been in the United States?"

I said, "This is our fourth day here."

"Oh wow." So, she gave me her number, and I gave her my nephew's number.

So, it went well. I had a very peaceful Christmas in a new country; I was so happy to have made it to the United States, even if my children weren't very happy. I said earlier that my wife had a relative and what had happened.

Chapter 5
California

I made a dream possible by bringing my whole family to the United States. Yes, I had a dream. I thought I mentioned it earlier, but I will mention it again. Honestly, I would have liked to live in my country and stay over there with friends and relatives. There were many other things I liked in Hungary. I also did a lot of work to make a nice life for my family. I worked very, very hard not to damage my kids the same way I was as a child. I was happy in my life as a child because I didn't know anything different. But after I married and had two children, I saw how much my kids were interested in the love of their parents and what it was to be a father giving hugs and attention. At that time, I found out what I was missing from my heart.

The hard work I did with Steve taught me a lot. If he had not stepped into and guided my life or had not seen me as a valuable boy or man — I don't know where I would be. After I had my kids and, as they got older, I realized what I got from him. Every day I understood what his wife did for me. I also saw that my uncle and his wife realized this boy needed attention, and they were like guardian angels to me.

These memories really hurt me, deep in my heart, and I had to hide it because I was unable to tell anybody. I didn't have a chance to say to Steve or to my uncle; I was going to tell people it was like a vacation. But really this was not a vacation, as I said in Hungary. But for me, I had a feeling after I came onto U.S. soil. We even had a hard and heavy winter in New York. I saw it had problems with the cockroaches.

But I knew my power, energy, and talent. I wasn't afraid to start a new life, this life, in this country. I wasn't able to speak any English. "Good morning." I knew that because the sun came up, and "Good evening," because the sun went down.

When I came to the U.S. with two children, my wife, we also brought my dog. It was my dog but closer to the kids. I know I was unable to bring anything else, just this dog, since it was very special for my two children and for me, too. I did not tell my wife it was very crazy for a dog, but she didn't say yes or no to that. She knew that I was trying to do my best.

I already mentioned when I came here, I immediately got Social Security. I would not start with a free lunch in the United States with two children. I stayed in Austria waiting to come to the United States. I got a job and saw to that on second day after I went to a motel, making sure the paperwork was finished. I was in Austria on a Saturday and then on the following Friday I went to a motel and waited to bring the whole family to the United States.

I made a little money and even over in Hungary I made a nice life for my children. But I didn't have any money because I was unable to bring any money from Hungary. I spent, of course, a lot of money living over there, even if many things were free. But it still cost money and, of course, the job did not pay a lot of money because I worked over there with some job.

For that reason, I came to the United States with $705. And then what has happened was I came to the United States in New York and as already I mentioned I was not looking for a free lunch. I immediately went to Social Security and then I worked because I knew the holiday was coming. I knew the kids needed a warmer shirt.

This man, as I mentioned, was able to give me a four dollars an hour job and add on the hours I worked by paying me six dollars an hour, even though it was on a holiday. Whether he was busy or not, he found a way for me to re-build an alternator, starter, and carburetor. He just knew in my country I was a very good auto mechanic for rebuilding alternators, starters, carburetors, and so many parts rather than going to a store and buying these parts.

He saw my expert work and the specialties for a car. He asked me, "Ferenc, what is your specialty when it comes to working on cars?"

I said, "Well, my specialty is, number one, Mercedes, and then, of course, I know Volkswagen and Audi. These are the three cars that mostly have manuals in Hungary. Steve had specialized in Mercedes, Volkswagen, Audi, and some Ford cars, but not many."

He found me and he said, "Well, Ferenc, I know there is one Hungarian guy here, and one German guy over at the Mercedes auto repair shop on the north end Boulevard in Brooklyn. I am going to talk to these people around the holiday and I bet he wouldn't mind hiring you."

He kept his word, and during the holiday he wanted to meet my family. He came to my nephew's apartment in Astoria. He was so glad and to meet my family. On Christmas Day, he helped me attend a Hungarian Catholic Church in Manhattan. This Catholic Church had a kitchen and cafeteria on the basement floor. After every church service, there was a little lunch. But on bigger holidays, it was possible to buy real Hungarian food.

He had a chance to talk to his friend, and I will never forget it. At that time, it was the 26th. After the holiday, it was a work day; a Tuesday. I went to work at his place. On December 27th, I met his friend.

He said, "Okay, Ferenc, show me what you're doing." He had one Mercedes over there. I would never forget that it was a 230 Mercedes. That one had a gas engine. He said, "It has a problem and needs a tune up. And, for some reason, the car had a problem with takeoff. You need to figure out what is wrong and fix it."

I checked the car and let him know what was wrong on the car in about fifteen minutes.

He said, "Are you serious? You found what was wrong that fast?"

I said, "Of course, I am serious."

What had happened was he ordered the parts and then I had the parts in a couple hours. He was in one place on the north end Boulevard, but also had a Mercedes dealer. He got the part from them. We did not need a long time to get the part, so I fixed the car in a couple hours.

He ordered what I told him. I used all the parts and then of course it came out in beautiful running condition.

He said, "Well, I think this guy mentioned a brake problem. Do you know how to repair this problem in that garage?"

Of course, I knew. The garage had a lift so he put the car on the lift. I took out the front and rear tires. I said, "Well, this car will need a rotor and brake shoes."

He said, "Are you sure?"

I said, "Of course, I am sure. I'm positive."

He ordered the parts, and then I changed the front and rear brake shoes and the rotor. He said, "Wow. It looks like you really know what you're doing." He also had a 1965 Mercedes 200D. He said, "Well, that car is not in running condition. It was towed here and has some problems."

I saw that the Mercedes had a problem with the timing chain. I checked it out. I tried to start the car, and then said, "That car has a problem with the timing chain. It has jumped." The man was lucky he did not damage the valve, but there was a 99% chance there was damage made on the cylinder head and the valve. But there was no damage yet in the rear. I said, "He's lucky if there is no damage made on the piston."

He said, "Well, we'll need to take it someplace to work on the engine."

I said, "No, no, no. Don't take it out. I'll take out the cylinder head if you want it now."

He said, "What do you mean? That is a big job."

I said, "It doesn't matter. I can take out the cylinder head in a couple of hours."

He brought tools over there. Of course, a Romanian/Hungarian man had come to his shop to see what I was doing and how I knew how to work on a car. He let me use his tools because I had nothing. I didn't know how I pronounce his name; it was Arpad. The man in the shop had a name that was easier to pronounce. His name was Steve or István. He had a same name as Steve in Hungary. He let me use his tools because he knew I had been in the United States for less than two weeks.

I took out the head; it had the exact problem I said.

He said, "Well, we need take out the cylinder head to have it repaired and put in a new valve. And then we'll get the rebuilt head in and put it together."

I said, "What are you talking about? Just go ahead. I checked out the cylinder head. There is no damage of valve seat. Go ahead. Order it."

One was completely broke, but I ordered it out. The man was lucky his timing chain hadn't jumped at a high speed; one valve was broke, but none of them were bent.

I said, "It's up to you how much you want to replace, the other one or just what has the damage."

He said, "I am going to talk to the customer on how much money he wants to spend." He said, "Well, might as well, because he likes this car. He wants to replace all the valves."

So again, he ordered the parts, and in a couple of hours he got the parts — the seal valve and everything. The next day I already had all the parts and took the cylinder head and fixed the valve seat and everything to fit a new valve in the old cylinder head. I thought I might as well change the valve guide. Mercedes had a copper valve guide and it could be taken out and, in a special way, put in a new one. I did everything and put that together. On the third day, the car was already running.

This guy said, "Well, you do not speak English. Well, for me, I don't care. Do you want to work here at the front doing service work or in the back to start rebuilding engines?"

I told him I knew how to rebuild transmissions, too.

He said, "Okay," and offered me a job. I worked for him for thirteen dollars an hour which was a big change in a short time.

But the sad part came now. Again, something was always sad and this was what I meant, because I already had a nice job that paid a lot of money, and he was so nice to me. He had the same nice name as Steve, and his partner was a German man whose name was Smit. In Austria, I learned how to speak German, so I didn't have a problem. He did not speak very much Hungarian, but he was able to pick up a couple words. The Hungarian and German language helped me talk to him.

But it was not really necessarily because of Steve; we discussed everything needed to do major things. I did not go over there, and he did not want to pay me for talking about something. He wanted to see how I was working. He did not want a person telling some story. I liked to work and start a car as soon as possible and finish it.

So, back to my family, since my family, of course, still didn't like my nephew's apartment. They didn't like the crazy weather and my dog was afraid of everything. My kids cried. My wife's cousin bought tickets immediately for the family to go to the Oakland airport on January 15th. My heart was broken because I had gotten a good job and loved to work on cars. The owner spoke my language, so everything was very good.

But I never wanted to leave my family. "I like my job, and then you guys, you like it or not it. If don't like, then it's too bad."

For me, number one, I only wanted to see my family was happy. I knew that, in California, one way or another way, I would make it happen by working and doing what I needed to do.

My wife's family picked me up at the Oakland airport and took me home. They were a nice family. Her husband was nice, and it was great to meet him. I find out immediately the city in north California didn't have any Hungarians or any shops owned by Hungarians.

There was one German guy looking for a partner or somebody to work for him.

My wife's cousin's husband said, "Well, this man's business is not very good. I don't know if he's honest or not. And mostly people are not starting to work."

He didn't know me well, but then I did not start working in an auto repair shop. I needed to work daily in auto repair, and he wanted to give me, after I repaired the car, half and half.

I said — his name was Dennis — I said, "Dennis, I know what I'm doing here. He's offering me a job. He picks up a car to repair. I don't need to know too much English, plus he's German. He speaks German, and then I speak about 50% German. But he is going to talk to the customers, and I'm going to repair cars." But it seemed to me he did not want me to start there.

I felt a little disappointed, so he took me to a wrecking yard to work and nobody understood or spoke my language. I needed to follow one guy, and we pulled out an engine of a car. He would point to it for me and I took out the whole engine. Guess what he paid me. He paid me $3.35 an hour.

I said, "Wow. It's okay. I'm not afraid to start or try something new to work on."

I worked there for about one week, but I did not speak English. I worked very well and made the owner very happy. Of course, I did not get any bonus money that week. I didn't matter how hard I worked. Because I didn't speak any English, I asked my wife's cousin's husband when I could ask Dennis for a raise. This time first I asked my wife's cousin, "Now I'm getting paid $3.35. How much money will I make monthly?"

Dennis said, "Don't worry. After four or five months, that maybe just half a year, you get a raise of fifty cents per hour."

I said, "Are you serious? So that means $3.85."

I did not speak English, but I knew what it meant in newspaper because I read what was for rent. I wasn't looking for a house for sale. I asked my wife's cousin, "How much is rent for apartments here?"

She said, "Oh, not very much. $400 to $600."

I counted how much money I made for a month based on an eight-hour workday for five days and a half day on Saturday. I told Dennis I made too much money to go on welfare. I would need to go on a street to get money from people to raise my family and live someplace.

Since it was not working very well, I met this lady in New York and then I called back. I also called back Arpad where I started to work. I told him what the situation was here. I talked to my wife and said, "I am very sorry, dear, but I don't have any other choice here. I have to go back to New York and make money. And then I will have money and go someplace else and not stay in north California in Redding because I am not going to able to do anything here."

Her name was Helen and her Hungarian name was Ilonka. I called her and talked to my friend Arpad who had the shop. He told me, "Ferenc, are you seriously going to California? A lot of people try to make it in California and almost everybody comes back." He said, "You were here with to two kids and already had a well-paying job. I know in Astoria you wouldn't have problems with cockroaches; I could find you a nice place."

It seemed to me my wife was not sure. She was the one who definitely did not want to stay in New York. Her heart wanted to go to California because her cousin said:

"Oh, it's very nice and everything is just beautiful and green."

At that time, I did not tell my wife I knew it was green, too. But even though grass and leaves were green, I couldn't use them for money. It didn't matter how I was working in Redding, California. I could only make money to pay for rent. Where was the food and how did I take the kids to school? But I did it because she wanted it.

In Hungary, she did not tell me to do any of this. "I like to do that," because, over there, we had friends. She had what she wanted, but here in United States, she didn't have any friends and it had been a long time since she had seen her cousin. She didn't know the difference between working in Hungary and working in the United States. It was a very cold winter, too. I just had to work and wait to see what happened in a couple of weeks or months.

There was a lot of people living in New York with the cold weather, and nothing happened. But it started that way where she was, day in and day out, hour after hour, not happy. It would break my heart if I saw an unhappy family. For this reason, I had to make it over there and try to do my best.

I talked to Helen. "I'm going back; my family is staying with our sweet cousin."

Helen said, "No, no, no, no. Don't come back to New York."

Arpad did not say that. He said, "You're welcome back anytime. So just come back, come back. Because you just work a little bit for Steve and he said this is just like a dream." Because nobody finished anything for him this fast and very few people knew that much about cars.

But I had a good, basic foundation because Steve worked on cars fifty-seven years and knew it very well. I was just fourteen years old and finished year eight in elementary school when I started working on cars. He was very nice to me; he was a very smart person who knew what he was talking about.

Helen – when I met her December 24, 1983 on Christmas Eve – her brother was in Monterey, California and a Catholic priest. He had a nephew who was a doctor and had four Mercedes. He took care of women and helped deliver babies in the hospital.

Helen said, "He has four Mercedes; he is doing very well as a Mercedes dealer at Star Motor in Monterey. His wife is a patient to them and his daughter and the whole family."

So, then this happened and I explain everything to her. She called from New York to Monterey and talked to her brother. Her brother immediately agreed. – I never forgot that. I talked to Helen and, of course, New York and California had a three-hour time difference. It was much earlier timewise in California. She finished the conversation with her. She called me and said, "My brother will call you pretty soon."

There was no call. I was waiting and waiting. I just finished talking. At that time, there were no cell phones. I finished talking to Helen and then the phone rang.

Father Doman said, "Oh, hi, Ferenc. How are you doing? In my heart, I feel I've known you a long time." Immediately, he wanted to pray with me on the phone. He said, "Because I am unable to reach you on the phone, we have already checked the Greyhound bus. You just need to decide what day you want to come down and then go to a Greyhound bus station to buy the ticket. In Redding, California, you need to go to the Greyhound bus station. He will ask for your name and when you're ready to come to Monterey."

I said, "Wow."

At this time, I did not want to talk to my wife. I just agreed. But I told him, "Okay, I would like to ask my wife a couple questions and let you know. But please don't hang up the phone because I will tell you immediately." I told my wife, "Dear, I got a job. It pays much better and will be an opportunity. What I mean is that I am talking to somebody. And he said, 'When you come down, you have a job immediately. I guarantee it. And then pretty soon you can make something here for your family and then bring them down.'"

She did not say anything. I couldn't tell if she was happy or not. She didn't have a chance to discuss this with her cousin.

Father Doman said, "Okay, we are going to the Greyhound bus station and pay for the ticket."

Not the next day, as it was a Friday, Dennis came with me on Saturday to a wrecking yard and explained to them that I needed to go down to Monterey. I was getting a job over there with higher pay.

Sunday, I went down and he paid me. I didn't speak any English. Dennis translated everything so I got my money and he helped me go to a bank to cash the check. On the next day, Dennis took me to the Greyhound bus station. I went down to Monterey.

The Catholic priest and one other man, his secretary, was waiting for me at the Greyhound bus station. I went over there and he took me to the auditorium where four priests were living. He said, "Just don't get lost. Walk around to see how you like Monterey."

I couldn't lie. Of course, everything was very nice. It had flowers.

I went back to the building.

They were asking me, "How do you like it?"

"It's nice," I said.

And then he brought me over to one window and pointed to the ocean and looked at it. He said, "The view is great by the bay."

I said, "Well, everything seems to be nice, Father." I said, "Father, everything looks good. But really everything would look good if I had work to do and able to start work Monday or Tuesday."

He said, "Wow. You really you want to go fast."

I said, "Of course, I don't have money and I have two children. I don't want to miss my two children that I love. My wife, she is there too. She's okay and the kids are too. But it doesn't matter how nice a place it is over there to stay in." Her cousin's house was private with four bedrooms, which was a pretty good size house. It had a swimming pool and everything. But when you didn't have money, it didn't matter how nice a place was.

Monday afternoon at 2 o'clock, he made it possible to meet with a Hungarian. His name was Steve again, Steve Lonhart. He worked for American Water District Company. He said, "Well, Ferenc, what do you know how to do?"

I said, "Well, I am an auto mechanic, but I specialize work on Mercedes cars. I also know how to paint and what is needed to remodel houses."

He said, "Oh, painting is same in Hungary as well as working on cars. But remodeling is a little bit different because of codes. You need to learn codes for this country." And then he said, "But really if you know what you're doing, I can help you." He asked, "How much English do you speak?"

I said, "Still, it's zero. I just know 'hi' and 'bye'."

He said, "Well, it's okay. But it seems to me you're a nice guy, you've proven with your two hands, and we'll talk."

On Tuesday, he took me to his nice house, and he also had one rental house. At that time, he was changing tenants. The place was empty – a very cute, small house. He said, "Okay, Ferenc, you need to paint this small house. There is work to do inside, but we will see how you are paint the house first."

He showed me. He took me to M&S Lumber Yard. At that time, we didn't have a Home Depot or Home Base or anything like that. He bought everything. He actually had a roller, but he bought the paint and a couple other things. He took me back to the small house. Actually, he lived in Monterey, but the small house was in Pacific Grove.

I started to work on the house. He already had a ladder over there and then I scrapped the fascia board. He told me what color of fascia board and what color of house he wanted. He said, "You are not going to get that far painting the fascia board today. This is the color for the fascia board. That is the house paint."

I was a very ambitious person. I wasn't afraid of work and almost jumped on the ladder. I did not jump on the step. I took three steps at once to be faster to go up to scrap the fascia board and spackle it and fix the cracks. I really knew how to paint. In Hungary, I did my house and parents' house. Even when I was ten years old, I painted my parents' house, the inside, and so many things. So, I was okay.

I spackled everything and it was nice, warm, better, and dry. I said, "Well, it's dry; I sanded it lightly to match the spackling the fascia board groove. What can I do?"

He told me he wanted to put primer on the fascia board.

I said, "Well, I remember he said the paint is in the paint house. What is primer?" Then I said, "Okay, I remember he pointed to the primer because it's the first coat." I primed it off the fascia board. I saw many cracks on the house. He bought once case of caulking. I fixed the crack. I caulked the window around and caulked the mantle and a thing I saw that a door jamb had a big crack over there and then it was not necessary to wait for plaster or stucco material. The caulking still covered it. Just one thing was missing. I didn't have a sponge and then I was looking around and finally I found one shirt in the garage. It had a very small, cute garage. I used the shirt. I caulked it and then made the caulking match the stucco. I did it.

The house was about a couple like an L-shape is stucco and the rest of the house was siding. I did everything and then the day was gone and he was working for the California Water District Company as district engineer. He came about 4:30, and, I will never forget: he came back and he said, "Are you crazy?"

I said, "Oh my God. What did I do wrong? What? Please don't fire me. What did I do wrong? Why are you calling me crazy?"

He said, "How in the hell were you able to finish that much? Did you eat lunch in two seconds or were you running around working? Look at it all the work you accomplished in a small amount of time. Were you looking for me to see if you were doing okay?"

I said, "Well, Steve, I was not looking for you or at the time. I enjoy this fresh, salty air in Monterey, actually Pacific Grove. I can't tell you how happy I am to work on that house."

He said, "Well, I can't believe you did not ask me. I'm not asking you either because it's only the second day. I don't know how to ask how much you want an hour."

I said, "Well, Steve, I don't know what I would say. I mean, I don't know how much I need an hour."

He said, "How about I give you $10 cash?"

I said, "Are you serious? You are going to give me $10 cash, after I work more than eight hours?"

He said, "You work as many hours as you want."

I never forgot.

He said, "Okay, going down the street has one place. I'll call it a Burger Barn." At that time, it had actually an uphill food store, grocery store, in that same parking spot. Maybe today, it had a Burger Barn there. He took me there, but we had a huge hamburger and big order of French fries.

At that time, I was so hungry because I mostly drank water all day. I did not tell Steve I did not know anything about a store being here. But even I knew the store was around the house. I didn't think I had money to go to buy food. He did not really know I didn't have any food. But it didn't matter. He bought a huge lunch and some other stuff for himself, too.

He was so happy and hugged me. He said, "I don't know why I have this feeling, but it seems like I have known you my whole life." He said he was so happy to meet me. He took me back to the Father Doman's house auditorium. He said, "Here is the most special man I have ever met in my life." He said, "Yes, he fixed the crack, put primer on the fascia, and the area what he caulked with primer and the house is ready to start to paint tomorrow. And then I thought he would finish it this week and the next week he was going to paint it. Only, he did this one because he bought everything he needed for this house." He said not because he thought I finished everything in a couple of days. He didn't have time to go back and forth to the store.

Father Doman was so happy. He said, "It's okay if you work that way. You have a lot of work here." He took me back the next day. At that time, I was not going to kill myself, but I painted the whole outside of the house. I even finished earlier, like 4:30. He finished his job at 4:00 and some days when he was very busy he didn't have time to come over to check what I was doing. He came back and the house was already painted.

The only thing left to do was the paint on the trim and the fascia board needed to dry. The third and a half day I finished the trims, door, and fascia board. Then at that time he was able to make it. He came back around 12:00. I would never forget he came back about quarter to 2:00. I found a rake and cleaned around the house nicely. Almost like an appointment, I finished everything to paint the fascia board, the trim, cleaned around the house, and put everything that was junk in a pile, and then sprayed a bit around the house with water. Everything looked brand new.

When he came over he said, "Oh my God. This? Where did you come from? What? Are you Superman or what?"

I was so happy. I said, "All right. God found a place for me."

This generation came from Hungary in 1956, so they lived in Monterey for many, many years. I already mentioned earlier there were about 500 immigrants in Monterey, mostly from the 1956 generation, and mostly everybody was about fifteen years older than me.

He took me there to introduce us. Her house needed a lot of work. At this time, we discussed what she wanted. Steve explained to them what a nice job I did outside. I had already done the outside paint job.

He said, "Well, I didn't know if I wanted him to paint the inside of the house, but I let him paint this little house."

I painted inside and then it had tile. The bathtub around had tile. He did not tell me to do that, but I scraped it all. It had a grout problem. I scraped out the bad grout and painted the bathroom and finished everything. It was not nice, but not really bad either. He just wanted to see how I did it. So again, I amazed him with the job.

It had come to a happier place for my heart. He said, "I don't care, Ferenc, if you're working ten or fifteen hours, it's up to you. You can work as many hours as you want."

But I said, "Yes, I can work all the way to midnight, but I need to go home," because at that time I didn't have a car.

He said, "It's okay to work on finding some solution for a car."

The lumber yard was still open. I went to him and asked to buy the grout and I brought a sample color of grout and more caulk for around the bathtub. The next day I went back in about noon, and then it was finished. This Hungarian lady and her husband came over to look at it – outside and inside of the house. They were so happy and hugged me. They said, "My God, it's a God-send you're here. You are doing a great job. Pretty soon you will make money, pretty good money, and bring the family down to Monterey."

Everything went so well. Only, it was very painful because I missed my child and family. Already a week was gone. He had a second wife and a stepson. His stepson lived in Cupertino and his wife's parents lived in Redwood City. His family had a Volkswagen Vanagon and gave it to me. It had a problem with its engine; it was leaking oil badly. But when I was about to start the car, I saw what was wrong.

At that time, the DMV was not open, so Steve said on Monday his son would take care of the paperwork and pay the registration. He took me to State Farm Insurance. I did not mention earlier, but I took a test for a driver's license with a Hungarian tape recorder in northern California, Redding. I already had a driver's license. Steve helped me take care of the insurance, so I got the sticker for the car.

At that time, the car didn't smoke yet. I think that started after a couple years when the car started smoking. But I didn't think it made smoke. We took it down to Monterey and I figured out it needed a rebuilt engine. I did that. It was called a Western Volkswagen. And again, Steve helped me to order the parts. I forget, but it was about a couple of days before we had the parts.

There was this lady, Elizabeth, and her husband's name was Joe; Joseph, but he was called Joe in United States, otherwise he called himself Yanosh, which was almost like Joseph

My name is Ferenc, but in the United States I started using Frank. Ferenc is the same as Frank in English. At that time, I always had a difficult time explaining what the name Ferenc meant and where it came from. Some people thought I came from France, Poland, or Russia. Nobody thought it was Hungarian. I started using Frank and people would call me Frank, but my legal name is Ferenc — Social Security card, driver's license, and everything.

I did pretty well on finishing off on this friend's house. I had a little money and was able to work on the car. It was very easy to rebuild a Volkswagen engine and change it. I fixed it in a couple days and then I had a running car. The following weekend, I had a surprise for my family. I did not say anything. I just drove up to northern California. That was 320 some miles one way, or about 640-650 miles back and forth.

I drove over there. The bottom of the Volkswagen Vanogan was blue and the top was a white color. Oh my God, oh my — my heart was almost broken. I had not seen my children for a couple of weeks so to see them from the car with everybody jumping around, jumping in the car, my son and my daughter was wonderful.

Here is a sad part. Again, my wife's cousin was not happy at all, especially Dennis. I had an extremely nice Volkswagen van. As I already mentioned, another Hungarian family had an Oldsmobile Delta 88 and it had low mileage. The lady was old and could not drive the car anymore. I already knew I was going to get that car for my wife. But even I had a hard time hiding that from my wife and kids. I said, "Not enough has happened. See here, I have a car."

Father Doman had already been talking about one house. I explained a bit to my wife that pretty soon we would have a house. It would need to be remodeled because the house had been vacant for a couple years. And then I went back and drove over to northern California on a Saturday and wanted to go as far I could.

I left around 5:30, 6:00 on a Sunday.

Steve Lonhart told me, "It's better if you leave a bit late and avoid traffic because a lot of people go up to Mount Shasta, and then on the way back to the Bay Area. There was pretty strong traffic." He said it would be better if I left around 6:30, 7:00 and I would make it close to midnight in Monterey.

I didn't have a GPS. Steve put the name and directions on a piece of paper and map, how I needed to go to make it up north and back to Monterey. I did okay. I made it. I didn't have any place to miss or go the wrong way. I better not go the wrong way because I didn't speak English.

On Monday, Father Doman and one auditorium secretary took me to one empty house that was at 543 Hannon Street. It was okay. It was a nice house. I was not going to call it a cute house. It had two bedrooms, one bathroom, carport and a garage – one car garage – and a pretty good size backyard. It had a red barn house. It was nice, but the house definitely needed a lot of work, inside and outside, topside, downside, everywhere.

Some bad people lived there and used the bathtub and corner for a toilet. The house was in very bad shape. Steve, again, took me to a Sherwin Williams paint store and introduced me to one Hungarian man who bought one of those stores. He said, "Anything you need, you come here because there are three Sherwin Williams stores: one in Monterey, another one in Pacific Grove, and Seaside has another Sherwin Williams. They don't have any others. I saw a Kelly-Moore, but for some reason there were three Sherwin William stores."

Father Doman's house, but Steve took me to a paint shop to get all of the materials and auditorium paid it and has a contract over there. Originally, somebody donated that house to the auditorium, but there were very bad people that lived in there before. Even after I finished the house and I lived within at least a year, the FBI was looking for people there. So that was a bad house.

I said, "I don't care." And then I cleaned it.

Of course, Steve bought me gloves. He said, "Here are special order suit. You pick it up when you start to clean it." Then he ordered the dumpster and I just took out the carpet and put everything in the dumpster. He bought a little spray can and said, "Just spray everything." He bought one kind of chemical and a smoke bomb in killing the fleas in the house. In the backyard, I found two to three-gallon buckets of needles.

I finished everything in a month and again, my wife was not working and the kids went to a school in northern California. I went up at that time on a Friday afternoon, and then I stay over there until Saturday and Sunday and helped over there. I had a plan to go back to Monterey on Sunday, but I saw that my wife and her cousin were not very happy. They saw I had a very nice van and I explained to them how nice everything was going here even though I did not speak English. I had a Bank of America checking account and then already got the checkbook, but I did not use it because I didn't know how to use it. But I had cash. I knew even she was asking me that or not, but Dennis said, "I hope you clean the house before you leave."

I asked my wife, "Are the kids going to school on Monday? Before I leave, I'm going to clean the house nicely."

Northern California had a paint store. I got over there to buy a special chemical to clean the dog because my family made it dirty. I told my friend at the store to talk to the manager and the paint store manager was not able to rent a carpet shampoo machine. He was so nice to me. He took me to Hodges Rental to rent a carpet cleaner.

Even Dennis – he had a shoe repair shop – was not home. He and his wife, my wife's cousin, worked together in the shoe shop. I shampooed the carpet and cleaned the dog with a special detergent. I waited for my wife's cousin and her husband to come home. I had a big surprise.

Dennis said, "My God, you cleaned the house and I have a very cute clean dog."

I said, "Well, because I shampooed the carpet."

He said, "What? You shampooed it?"

I said, "Yes, I did."

"How did you get cleaner?" He called to this paint store. "I already saw that immediately it was very easy to get a place called the Westwood Village and it was not too far from your wife's cousin's house. Hodges Rental was just across the street from that."

Everything went well to pick up a carpet cleaner and take it back. It was nothing because my Hungarian friend talked to a man and helped me one time.

I finally left his house and because I went to that guy there had food store, a Holiday food store actually. Northern California had many stores called "Holiday". I had a nice dinner and everything. They made Hungarian paprikash, plus Dennis liked steak and I knew that already. I bought a beef chunk to make a steak dinner. He had the barbeque and then I had the paprikash. I made the Hungarian paprikash.

He said, "Well, I hate to ask you, but you said you are already making money. Can I have some money because your family is here and eating all of our food?"

I said, "Okay. Oh my God. Okay. It's no problem." I never wanted a free lunch, but I was glad I had money and even gave him a surprise. My daughter remembered I needed to write the check. And so, I wrote a check to him.

When I paid him $600 and then I knew I had all that money in the checking account, and he almost stopped breathing. I said, "Okay, here's a check for $600."

He said, "Whose check is that?"

I said, "My check. Steve already helped me open a checking account at Bank of America."

I took everything to my family. I had a new car and an old house. I made the inside extremely cute. Outside, was a flat roof, small house. To me, it was cute and nice. I painted it inside and outside. I put in new carpet and new linoleum in the kitchen. I changed it to a Formica kitchen counter and everything was just ready to go.

I still saw my wife was a little bit homesick, and still had tears in her eyes, and she said, "Ferenc, you always make me happy feeling surprise. I just can't believe you worked so hard. You fixed a car. You painted the house. You came up this weekend to visit us and then you make a house like that." She knew nobody else did it. I did it. The auditorium helped me to paint over there and then everything came out very well.

In Monterey, Steve Lonhart was working for an American. I did, back and forth, work to one Hungarian family to go to work with another Hungarian family. Steve was working in the California American Water Company. He had one friend there who wanted to add another bathroom on his house and one bathroom/bedroom and a little living room. The living room had a kitchen area. The downstairs had a living room and bathroom and the kitchen looked like when you go inside a studio. But it had a good-sized bathroom. Not like a studio, but it looked like it. This happened and the upstairs had another bathroom – a pretty good-sized bathroom and small – and a large closet and for some reason just had a half bathroom with no shower.

I met another Hungarian guy and he was a contractor. He did some foundation work because that was really neat to know somebody who knew how to do a foundation to code. He showed it to me and he had employees. He had one son and we worked with him, and he spoke Hungarian. He showed me how I needed to code to pass inspection for a foundation and a couple of serious codes.

I did this work to start and then pour concrete. What came out was pretty good. And then it was finished, and he helped me because it had a raised foundation – to do the first floor to a joist, to put it on joists, king beam and a joist and plywood. I put that into the floor. I knew very well how to read a house plan, and then I did construction in Hungary. Of course, codes and everything were different.

Steve came over. That house was not too far from the place he worked and his friend or partner worked at the California American Water Company. He came home and checked to make sure everything was fine and how he needed to make the stairs and the header to a window – 4 x 12 someplace or 4 x 8.

Of course, it was not an overnight job. But I was a person who liked to learn new things and was pretty fast. I went to electrician school in Hungary, but just an electric engineer. As an auto mechanic, you need to know how to make a plan for an engine and everything. So, I was very, good at reading house plans.

I finished this construction and it came out extremely nice. I would never forget. I didn't speak English still. At times, I said zero was what I spoke because I was working and I didn't have other people to talk to. I didn't have time to go to a school to learn English because I needed money for going to the next step to doing things.

The inspector came and checked everything. I followed him and he checked and he shook his head. He hit his knee and saw something and I didn't know what he was talking about. I went to another thing and saw he marked on one paper and then I didn't know. At first, I thought *Oh my God, I did that much wrong*. But I couldn't say anything because I didn't speak English.

He almost finished inspecting the house and the electric work. His name was Nolan. He came over with Steve.

I told Steve, "I don't know what is wrong with this inspector, but I can't figure out if he's mean or I am doing that much wrong. He always pats his knee or says something." He went over there to talk to the inspector.

But the inspector was on his way to Steve and Nolan to talk to them. "Who did this construction?" He came over two or three times to check before the sheetrock covered everything on the building and he never found anything wrong. He said, "How come he did everything? I'm unable to mark one thing that isn't good. And then and he doesn't speak. It's not that he speaks bad English, but he doesn't speak English at all. He's not from here because he told me two or three times, 'Hi, good morning.' But I would ask him something and only one thing he could tell me back was, 'I'm sorry. I don't speak English.'" Steve said, "You know why because he did everything on the house plan and did it exactly how you guys signed the paper." He said, "You're right."

So that came out pretty well. I always say some people don't like to put it in a book this name but I think I have power. I have power and I am extremely ambitious. In my picture of my family, especially my two kids, it's my dream to not spoil it but do everything to make it happen for them to go to a school and have the education and skills they want to learn because I didn't have this choice. The only way I could do auto repair school was because of Steve in Hungary. He hid it and he took me to a school because he saw I was a person who needed help.

There came a time where Steve said, "Ferenc, something interesting has happened. In Monterey County, they have a water plan, a big one where water is coming from a dam but because it has a lot of forest fires, the dam needed to be cleaned up. But the filter plant was very old. It was built in 1947 and it was time to do a complete reconstruction to take out all the valves – what was the old valve – and put in a new plastic valve. But, mostly, a lot of pipe was not going back to it. Not galvanized, not copper. It's going to using a plastic pipe.

He said, "That's an extremely big job what needs to be done, and pretty it should be good money. You think you're going to do it?"

I said, "Of course, I will do it. How much concern is there on time to complete the job? Does it need a posted date to finish it? Or if you finish it one month later, it's okay. It's still okay."

"Of course," he said, "if it's two months later, everything is still okay."

So, he helped me get a special license and insurance to work in California. He hired me as a contract job and not as an employee. I got the license, insurance, bond, and everything to finish this job for the California American Water District.

I had this small house and it had a carport and a garage. I emptied the garage and made it ready to deliver the material. There were a lot of parts and pipe and fitting that needed to be cut onsite. It had a big tank filled especially with sand and ash. It was like a filter system in a tank and that tank was fifteen feet high and eighty feet long.

In order to take out all the old piping and put in back a new special pipe, he hired a Hungarian contractor, Jimmy. Everybody called him Jimmy. He did that so I did all the plastic fittings and plastic that went inside the tank and then put in a special way to clean out the tank if necessary after the water was filtered out. It had a bit one-way sand – one type of sand, one type of rock or another type of sand, another. It had about twenty layers in the tank to clean the water that came from Nacimiento Dam. It depended on the tank – to shut the system down or clean it automatically. This was an unusual thing.

Because Steve helped, me it was not necessary at all to speak English. I was able to survive only on my language. I finished everything and then it was hard to believe it but the first year I did a whole job in about nine months. I did a lot of tanks. I did sixteen tanks, which was a lot of work. It was amazing how much work it took to do it but I got $165,000. That was very nice money to start.

I got this money. Steve said, "Well, Ferenc, I don't know what you want to do with this money, but I know there is one house here for sale. Are you interested in buying it on Franklin Street?"

That Franklin Street and David Street corner had this house but there was no foundation. It had a house. Well, used to be just a fisherman's house. It would be to buy to have and no foundation – a foundation sitting on redwood 6 x 12, 10 x 12 and that was it. But on the front of the house, somebody did before sometime put on a little foundation and 2 x 4 bar.

It meant the house did not need complete construction just like remodeling. Steve was an engineer. He knew very well what he was talking about. He said, "Ferenc, why don't you just buy this house?"

I bought the house for $85,000 cash. No mortgage. I got $85,000. He knew this was the lowest price I could afford. But the house around it had only three feet. No lot size. It was almost just the size of the house. Around the house in the front had about five feet to the curb and on the side, it had three feet barely. The backyard had eight feet. So that was all. Of course, no garage.

But Steve showed me an opportunity by going up the roof and we saw an extremely nice view of Monterey Bay. He said, "Here, some people can see the ocean just fine and buy the house immediately." He knew that and he told me, "Don't dream to move in this house. Just remodel it and fix what needs to be done – the foundation, everything – and then sell it because you're going to sell the house at a very high profit."

So, I did not fight with him. I took his advice and I bought this house.

But, of course, it was still in my blood to work on cars. Also, some Hungarians had over there a Volkswagen, Audi. Three of them were Mercedes dealers. I did work a little bit to a little routine. I saw that winter had come. Of course, there was no snow over here, but it was the rainy season. I decided this house needed a foundation and so many other things. I did it slowly, even though I had plenty of money to do it without loans to buy the material to do the construction. But I couldn't take it out in my mind or heart to not work on cars.

What had happened was Steve Lonhart and Father Doman took me to Star Motor and introduced him and that time I spoke a little bit of English, but not much. He introduced me and said I had a lot of experience working on cars, especially Mercedes.

He said, "I don't care if this man speaks English or not. You think he knows what he's doing?"

I told Steve to say, "Of course I know."

And he said, "Okay."

He had probably fifty engines in the backyard in one shed – engine, transmission – but not in the shop, just engines almost all the way to the door to the back wall. There was a pile of engines, but they were piled nicely. It was not just dumped or dropped over there. Just never know what has happened with this engine. Rebuild that, fix that, or someday.

Many engines just change because Monterey, Carmel – especially Monterey, Carmel, Pebble Beach – had a lot of Mercedes and Volkswagen, BMW. But if you were to drive around in Caramel or Pebble Beach, I'm talking about out of ten cars that you see, you would see about seven or eight would be Mercedes.

It had a lot of cars. I didn't know how many were here. The engines were piled. He said, "Well, are you interested? Your choice, and you know what you're doing to rebuild that. Go ahead." He cleaned one room on that huge property on Star Motor and he had in the back of the room about 25 x 30. And then he said, "Make the room the way you want to do it and let me know what I need to buy what I need to do. We are going to do it to make it happen to have you rebuilding engines." He did not hire me as an employee. He did contract job piecework.

Using Steve's help, he put down the parts in my language and then in the English. He said, "You need to order the parts. You see that over there, Ferenc, where it says 'kit' or 'valve' you need to fix it. You circle it and then I have an order sheet. And then you circle it over there what parts you need by using this little paper like a dictionary."

It helped me learn English and came out extremely well. I had personal time and keying into this building, he didn't care if I was working at midnight or noon or Saturday or Sunday or Monday or up to me. He didn't care. I came very well to making money on that way also.

I still did paying jobs for roof jobs, tile roof, and new bathroom, replace a bathtub, everything. I remodeled houses various places. A husband or a son or somebody came from Hungary or a relative helped me to do it. I used my talent and my skill to do that remodeling. A relative gave me a hand to make it possible to lift up a wall easier. Many places in Monterey had a garage and convert the garage into a studio and rent it out about $800 to $1200 a month. I didn't know how many I did.

I saw on some property a small storage, a 10 x 12, with no permit. Not a floor, a 10 x 12 eaves. But I made very short eaves, so it came out really a little house where there was just a fascia board on the wall. On both sides I did a six-inch hangover roof. That way it came out to be sitting on a property of 120 square feet or 10 x 12.

I did a carport over there. I always had one other friend, Jimmy's son, had a pickup truck and he came over there to deliver it or sometimes people or-dered it, or sometimes it went to a U-Haul to order that trailer, and sometimes even a car and a trailer. Somebody wouldn't have a tow hitch and would bring it on his property. I would put that together on his property and made a fortune for that.

This was a lot of work. I miss a lot of my family. It started a bit of compli-cations in my marriage. Especially the first half there, I had an extremely hard time with my wife. She was homesick for Hungary and then she would cry be-cause she didn't have a friend. She had a friend, but she didn't have a hairstyling license. But in Hungary she did not exercise it very much to work on hair. She was unable to pick up any customers in Monterey without a license. Everybody had a license.

What happened was that people – it didn't matter if they were Hungarian, German, or Romanian – she still wasn't at home. A while back, she started to clean apartments and babysat. But for some reason, it did not come out okay. She never cleaned. She was almost never working in anything else except as a hairstylist.

A little more every day she was – to say – jealous or acting different to-wards our son and daughter. I don't know. She was a little sarcastic and she had lost friends in Monterey. I am not saying I was an angel or a special person myself. I did not say that.

A lot of people had called me a special person. Didn't matter if it came from the Iranian or the Italian in Monterey or I did a lot of work in Fisherman's Grotto. He came from Pakistan. But because I had extremely high skills for everything, I had a chance to work sixteen hours day, thirty-two hours a day.

But already I planned it like what I did in Hungary. If somebody worked someplace or they didn't have a job, but they knew a little what they are doing and then I extremely highly teach them, show them how they need to do it. That way it worked out well in Hungry for the right person. But it came out very well in the United States, too.

But she was not really an honest person and had a couple of friends. But it was very sad. She got a friend but became jealous because she was an extremely nice-looking lady. Some bastard people said, "How are you doing? Are you sure Ferenc is taking care of you?" But, of course, it was a man who did it. She was bored at home and a couple of friends she made came over and would drink coffee and stay home. She started to get used to somebody saying, "Oh, you're doing that one wrong."

I said, "I am doing something for somebody, and I'm working that many hours. It's not his business the way I am doing work for somebody. And if the person likes it, it's not somebody else's business whether I do it right or not."

A problem started a bit and a lot of women didn't like her nice life; she got to stay home, watch TV, and make lunch. She did not have to be at work like many other women. Because her husband came to my house and was drinking coffee and then a lot of wives didn't like that.

I agonized extremely. I needed to finish very well and have an extremely nice water plan. The California Water Company has a huge valve. We needed a meter and put in a valve underground. That underground hole or meter over there. This little underground had a tough time to go down deep about fifteen feet. Backhoe had come to make a big hole and then I had a special way to make a hole built with very strong rebar and cement floor.

It was special, but not as much a problem underground water, but you never know what will happen in the future. I did a special sealer to seal it to never have a problem with underground water. I built it with cinderblock. I'd never forget. I did it in Hungary. I used clay block in a little bit of construction but I had not worked very much with cinderblock. It was totally different than the clay cinderblock used in Hungary.

Steve Lonhart just came over there and he saw how I was using my two fingers to put the mortar in some area. He said, "This is an amazing job you're doing. But I'm telling you this time you are not really a brick layer."

I said, "Well, Steve, that stupid cinderblock is totally different than the clay. And it doesn't want to stick. I don't know how I put the mortar to stay over there."

He said, "Don't worry about it, Ferenc. You are doing an amazing job." And just one thing came very well with another thing.

What had happened was one Hungarian friend had a very old house in Seaside. Earlier, I met his son and daughter who were kids at the time, and they met my kids in school. Of course, everybody wanted to meet a new Hungarian family in Monterey. But his wife died.

He had a couple of houses but had one on a very big lot with one house. I found out the old house was torn down and it was possible to put in two houses. He needed to subdivide by changing the subdivision to building two houses. But in Seaside where this house was located, the second floor had an extremely nice ocean view to Monterey Bay.

Actually, a little bit back. Steve and I bought the house over there. But I bought this house in Pacific Grove and did so much work on it. It was hard to believe but. Honestly, I did that huge amount of work and I spent a lot of hours. But still I spent as much as I could with my kids. But since it started a little bit difficulty for my marriage, I did not always like to at stay home very much. I just wanted to be home when my kids were home and then close to the time when I would go to bed.

I still made it home at noon to eat and take a nap. But when the kids were in school, I would stay home mostly for a half an hour or one hour. But, at that time, I would eat quickly and take a nap usually for twenty minutes. I did this house besides doing many other jobs in Pacific Grove.

Actually, I think I said it was Monterey, but it was on the David and Franklin Street corner; on one side it was Monterey, and on the other side it was

Pacific Grove. I worked on the Pacific Grove side of the house. And then again, on one side, if I went up a hill to north the end, the left side was Monterey and the right side was Pacific Grove. Actually, I was sorry I said that. It was that small section called New Monterey and then down another five streets towards the ocean and then it changed to Pacific Grove. I didn't know why I did it that way, but it was okay. Now I made that clear.

I finished that house and then again, I would never forget that. I went to pick up more material but I was very close to finishing the construction – about a week to finish everything. I was looking for something and I saw over there a sign that was for sale by owner. I said to myself: *why not just pick up a sign that says for sale by owner?* I did it, and then I found one over there that was almost four feet, 2 x 2. I made it short on one side with a scale saw, staple it on a for sale sign on this stick, and then I put that on the front of the house. That was on a Saturday about eleven, or close to noon.

I was upstairs installing a bathroom faucet and checking the kitchen. Everything was very close to being done for an occupancy inspection.

In less than an hour, somebody said, "Hello, hello, hello? Is somebody here?"

I said, "Yeah, I am here."

They said, "Is this house for sale?"

I didn't speak very much English, but I understood what he said. I said, "Yes."

He said, "Can I speak with the owner?"

I said, "I am the owner."

He said, "You are the owner?"

I said, "Yes, I am."

He walked around, and the downstairs had, of course, no garage just a living room. The back room had two bedrooms – a small bedroom because second floor has extremely nice ocean view. I made the upstairs like a family room and one more bedroom and a kitchen. The whole thing was not very big, but it had everything. It had three bedrooms, a kitchen and a family room. Just only about 75% view to the bay. The reason for this was it had a view from the living room to the ocean, a kitchen, and even a one-bedroom window had pointed to a little bit to Monterey Bay and then upstairs and downstairs had a full bathroom. The only difference was the upstairs had a bathtub and downstairs had a shower.

The man asked me for a price and I saw he figured out he did not believe I was the owner. He said, "Who is the person I need to make a deposit to?"

I said, "How much do you want to pay?"

He said, "Whatever you ask me; I don't mind this price. I will make a deposit for the house."

At that time, I didn't have a cell phone; I had a phone, but no phoneline in this house. Steve lived not too far from that house. I said, "Well, please come back later at 4:30." I saw he was holding the "for sale by owner" sign and then he brought it inside. I said, "Well, okay. I'm not going to fight this person to not do it."

It looked like he was serious, so I explained the situation to Steve. We already discussed the price a bit and I told him the man offered more money for selling the house because I thought he would give the best offer. But he did not say anything.

Steve said, "Ferenc, it looks like he wants this house badly. Why don't you ask for another $25,000? I'm going to explain that to him. Why not just tell him, 'Okay, this is the price, but it's that much on that one coming on top of the house." And then he said okay.

He changed the check for Steve with a little higher deposit. He said, "Make the house $5000 deposit, not $1000, and then we're going to open escrow. We'll hold your check for thirty days and cash it if he changes his mind. It's okay." This was a cash buyer and he bought the house immediately. I sold that house pretty well.

Another house I stepped in was this Hungarian family's. I had money to buy this old house, plus in Seaside, the house was cheaper like Monterey. But I did not really care about whether it had an ocean view or not. I bought this house. I already mentioned earlier it needed a subdivision for two houses. I decided to build two houses.

One was a peach colored house and one house was a grey colored house. Same thing as the downstairs – it had a garage, a one car garage. It was a deep garage and then had an entry and after that it had a bathroom on the left side. There was garage on the right side had a closet and after that it had on the right. On one side – because it was hard to have each a right side/left side of the house – it had a bathroom, a full bathroom. Across this full bathroom had a room for a walk-in closet and a bedroom and had a hallway, and the left side had another bedroom. The bedroom closet was sticking out from the house and then above that I built a deck. It had a beautiful view to Monterey Bay.

I did the kitchen and the living room and the master bedroom. In the front above the garage, it had a master bedroom. It was a nice, large bathroom and across it had a kitchen. That had a walkway to a living room. The living room walked out to a deck and again, an amazing view to Monterey Bay. I did both houses identical. Only the house number was different, but the floor plan – to save money – was actually the same for both houses. The one house's color was pink and the other was peach.

This house was finished around the end of school. My family always went back to Hungary during the summer. After a couple years, we could not go back to visit in Hungary because immigrants were not allowed to go back. But we left in 1983, and the first time the family went back in '87, almost four years later we came to the United States in December and went back for the first time in June or July of '87. After that, my kids finished school on June 8th and then leave for Hungary on June 8th or June 9th. They would stay over there till the end of August.

I was always involved in construction and auto engine repair. I never went back to visit in Hungary; I extremely liked United States. I just always had a feeling I was on vacation. When I had a nice vacation, I didn't always want to continue day by day to the next day. Still, I dreaded it; I didn't want to go back there. I changed my heart to my land. From my heart, I said I was born in Hungary but now this was my country. My heart was here and I loved, to today, the United States. This was the nicest, most beautiful country. A lot of people didn't know the difference. I didn't understand why people complained here in the United States; they didn't know what was really bad. It didn't matter how many problems this country still had; it was the best in the world.

I stepped into other jobs. When my family left for Hungary, I lived in a very nice house. It was a small house but everything was nice. I couldn't say it was extremely nice construction, but the inside for an example, had a flat roof, gravel roof, and then a garage had a carport built in a very interesting way. But I liked it because it was peaceful and had no problems. It had everything I needed inside.

My family came back to Hungary and at that time I finished both houses and rented one house for somebody. I decided I was going to move into another house. So, I was bought everything new, such as a new washing machine. Before, I would pick up a washing machine from the street and then repair it, but it would usually break and wasn't worth fixing it. I would get another one from the street or from a friend who bought a new one and I would keep it in the backyard and then I covered it with tarp. Many times, a Hungarian family would know I had a washer or dryer, dishwasher. They were always asking me first before they bought a new one. But this time I bought a new washer/dryer, a brand-new TV, and a Kitchen Aid appliance. Both kids had a TV in their bedrooms and everything I bought was new.

I always had a Mercedes, but I had a chance to buy an Audi. Somebody was unable to pay immediately after they bought the car. One Hungarian friend's son was working as an Audi dealer. He called to tell me the car had a bit of damage on the right fender and rear. But the car only had 7000 miles and very cheap because the car had been hit. I bought that Audi. It even had a metallic blue sealer, like blue sealer car. It was only $5000 and a very nice car.

I got the Volkswagen Vanogen and then besides that because always I needed a pickup truck, I bought one using it for construction. As I mentioned early, one lady gave my wife an Oldsmobile Delta 88. That one was like brand-new and had very low miles, and it was a pretty good size car. That one I think was also metallic blue with a while leather top and a four-door car.

My family was in Hungary and I decided to buy my wife this Audi. The house was new and inside the house everything was brand-new. The car was not brand-new, but in good condition. Where it came from, nobody knew. I only went to the body shop to paint it the same color because the fender had to be painted to match it. There wasn't any difference because he used factory paint to paint it from a dealer. I changed the rear and the bumper, but the bumper came with same color as the car before in the factory. In that way, it was like a new car.

And then I drove it. At that time, I still had a Volkswagen Vanogen because it had more room to pick up everybody at the San Francisco airport. For many years, I had this Volkswagen Vanogen because it had a popup top for camping, even though I didn't have time to go camping. But sometimes people used it.

I went to the San Francisco airport to pick up the family. On the way home, I told the family – driving them in the Volkswagen Vanogen – "I'm sorry I forgot something over at the house. I'm not sure if I turned off the water. I need to check to be sure everything is okay."

I took the family to the new house. I drove up the driveway and then opened the garage door. I opened the garage and immediately the family saw the new Audi.

My daughter said, "Whose car is that?"

I said, "Well, somebody will be living in this house pretty soon and brought the car here." I was teasing. I was not lying to her, just teasing. I said, "Well, why not come in and look at the job I did inside?"

The kids came inside the house. I had already picked up some stuff for my daughter for her bedroom. My daughter was looking for me and said, "Daddy, why is my stuff in this room?"

I said, "I don't know. It looks like the person living in this house has the same taste as you."

My son went to the room on the left and said, "Oh, my stuff is here, too."

"Oh my God," I said, "these people probably came to our place and took a peek in your room. They definitely wanted to have what you have. Oh my God. Well, it looks like this man has a similar home as our house downstairs."

Going upstairs, I had bought all the new furniture. But it had one or two things. The china cabinet was almost brand-new and a table and a little chest. I brought it from another house.

At that time, my wife looked at that and said, "Don't tell me you're going to living in this house."

I said, "Okay, I'm sorry. I had a very hard time going that far. Yes, we are going to live in this house. It's paid for and I don't need to pay rent; it's a done deal."

Oh my God, my kids were jumping around and screaming and our dog was running around the room because we still had a dog. The kids were just so happy. I gave back the rental house to the auditorium. I lived in Seaside in a beautiful house. It had three bedrooms and downstairs there was a little garage. It only had room for one car in the garage. No room for a two-car garage, but it was an extra deep garage. It was like a normal garage but almost two feet wider without the room for two cars.

My family was so happy that we lived in that house for many years. I continued to do many auto engine repairs. I rented one shop and made a license, but it was not open exactly to the public. I built up customers and had somebody call me to make an appointment to bring their car over to work on because they needed me to do it. Still, today, I am buying cars, whether I need it or not. Mercedes – of course just Mercedes – to fix an engine or whatever to make myself happy.

For some reason, I couldn't stop because I made an extremely nice profit from construction. For example, you're not going to believe it, but sometimes I worked on Mercedes V8 engines. They had problems with the timing chain and in 1989 and 1990 they had a factory defected valve guide and sometimes the valve stem seal. It was not the best material, especially the valve guide had to be replaced and a weak timing chain on the Mercedes.

A lot of people could not believe it since they were thinking if they bought a Mercedes they would never need to touch it. But a problem would start depending on how much they used the car. A problem usually happened at about 65,000 miles to replace the timing chain. A lot of people did not replace it and chain would jump and it busted a cylinder. Sometimes I needed to replace the whole engine or just the cylinder head or change the valve guide, valve stem seal and valve seat, so it depended.

I will never forget when I started on a V8 engine 560SL Mercedes and especially the 560-aluminum block that came out and had this problem in it. But not just SL, but SEL or SE, all V8 engines had this problem. I did it straight for about twenty-seven months just working on my friends' engines and had to replace them or a complete engine.

I delivered a 560SEL Mercedes to Saratoga. A man was waiting for me, but he was cross. I said, "What is wrong? What has happened?"

He said, "Well, I have a contractor. He said he's coming to finish the marble work on the front of my fireplace and mantle. This is his third or fourth time and he's not showing up."

I said, "Show me what you're talking about." He showed it to me, and then I said, "Do you have the materials here somewhere?" The materials were there and everything he needed to do the job. I said, "Do you want me to do it?"

He said, "Don't piss me off. What are you talking about? You want to install it? You brought the car for me. You're working on the car and then you say you're going to install marble to the front of my fireplace?"

I said, "Don't worry."

He said he had everything but the tile.

I said, "Don't worry. I am coming back tomorrow."

He said, "No, no. I already planned it for today. I was just around to the tile store where they got the marble and I saw they had a tile saw for $168. I can rent it or buy it. I don't care. I just want to finish the job."

I said, "Okay."

I wasn't used to delivering cars all the time, but I did it because sometimes somebody wanted me to pick up his car to fix a cylinder head and the car was running. I always bought mechanic special Mercedes. It had a good deal and I would repair it. Then sometimes somebody's car broke down, then I load up to him what I had. I did pretty well. I fixed this guy's fireplace. We went to pick up the tiles. The contractor there – I didn't know if he was a contractor or the tile sealer – he showed up and went back.

The man asked, "What are you looking for?"

He said, "What do you mean? I'm here to do the tile job to start the work."

He said, "Well, remember when you said you were coming at eight? What time is it now? It's eleven o'clock. I changed my mind. I don't need you to do it. I bought the tile saw, and my auto repair guy is going to finish it."

This guy thought he was joking.

I talked to him to find out what he wanted. I finished about four hours later. I didn't know if I made another mistake or just sometimes I said a mistake but not really because I just got more work. I went from one marble job to another one and changed a kitchen. That time it was not granite. It was marble. This countertop first came out about the eighties, nineties. End of the eighties, '90, '92, '94 – I did a lot. I had one friend where I did so many years of construction. Like in Carmel really, I did a tile roof for this huge house with about 7000 square feet tile roof. It was a mansion and then I didn't know how many years I did tile roof.

At this time, my brother-in-law came from Hungary. Sometimes my cousin came from Hungary. My half-sister came to visit us, and then her husband helped me work on it. I met somebody. He did construction work in Monterey County and another place in Walnut Creek for a school district. He found me many places I did in schools installing a soundboard. For some reason, the school didn't have enough room. Remodeling was a major problem at the school and they bought this mobile building. Somebody put that building together. But on the inside the sound board needed to be put on the walls. It paid very well.

As an example, I did a job in Walnut Creek with my brother-in-law, my sister's husband. Because of traffic, I woke up at three in the morning like in Hungary when I had a dairy farm. I would make it there before traffic. But I had to leave earlier than six because of the extremely high traffic to pass through to go down to Monterey.

We went to work, and then I left and was home by 9:30, 10:00, and I would sleep a little bit and go back the next day.

I would never forget when my brother-in-law said, "I'm going back to Hungary and then I will explain to everyone you driving about 400-500 kilometer every day and Ferenc is working 6:30-7:00, 6:00 A.M. to 6:00 P.M. People will say, 'Okay, Lazio. Now at that place it might fly, but please don't try to come up with another baloney or don't lie again.'" Because he said people weren't going to believe how hard I was working.

But I was doing pretty well. I had one friend who lived in Carmel. He was married to one lady in Spokane, Washington. We wanted to drive. I did rebuilding. He kept the Caramel house, but his new wife had a house in Spokane, Washington. They wanted me to go over there and my brother-in-law – he was my wife's brother – was here visiting. So, we drove to Spokane in a car. He had another car to drive it back to Monterey and drop it in Carmel, so everything was a done deal. It looked wonderful.

I said, "Well, my wife's brother is going to see a lot and then I'm going to see what is going on over there." I drove it over there and, of course, I knew her husband very well for many, many years. I will explain a bit what had happened with him in Pacific Grove.

In Spokane, she had two houses because her mom had died. She said, "I have a nice basement, but obviously it's missing a bathroom. No bathroom but it has water and a washing machine in the basement. But I have always wanted to put one in. But you wouldn't mind putting in a bathroom downstairs in the basement, would you?"

I said, "Well, okay." I did it.

I measured it and checked out what needed to go in. That basement had a regular standard eight-foot ceiling. It had center drainage so I raised the floor up to about ten inches for a toilet. I cut the concrete a bit to lower the sewer pipe for a toilet and made a sink and bathtub. I made the bathroom. There was always something coming up.

While I was there, they took me to his mother house and same thing. Nobody lived in that house at that time. She said, "This bathroom has a problem leaking and the tile is loose on the wall. Please put in another, replace at least the tile."

I knew I had to start the tile. I saw that already the bathtub was not in decent shape and then it was cheap. It was a cast-iron bathtub because the bathtub was thirty-five or maybe forty years old. The plumbing had galvanized pipe. Monterey had bad water and a lot of houses had galvanized pipe. I made a fortune by replacing galvanized pipe with copper pipe.

I replaced a bathtub, the tile, and plumbing in the house. I stayed over there longer, and at that time, my wife was driving.

I said, "Hey, guys, you've started school break, so just come here." They came here and stayed a bit because it looked like this family did not want me to go back to Monterey.

I did not hide it. I really loved Spokane. It was an extremely nice city and nice people lived there. So, my friend's wife said, "Well, my mom and father had one piece of land next to the railroad." In the backyard, there was an old building. There was a railroad, but some not exactly a railroad next to a property because some odd shape lot or some piece of land over there. They had all this land. She said it was possible to put couple of houses over there. They went to the city to find out if it was possible to put on that piece of land six small houses — so not a six plex, but actually it was twelve units or six little houses.

Her name was probably Nancy. She said the house planning and the people were not crazy for like an apartment and that it was much better to build six small houses. At that time in Spokane a place not far from an army place over there. The army did was very well in Spokane. The house market was crazy over there. You put down a house at 8:00 in the morning and by 11:00 it was sold.

I designed it and checked it, and in California it was called mixed lumber. Mixed lumber had a special package house. It came with 1060 square feet or 1268 square feet. There were three bedrooms, two-car garage, and one bathroom and one floor. The laundry room was in the garage. So, if I added on another four feet, it had three bedrooms, two bathrooms, and a laundry room in a garage. Otherwise, it was one bathroom and a laundry room inside the house and add on a little bit a garage and a house. Add on four feet on the side one side. That came out 268 square feet.

I built a house over there because coming up in the house everything was cut inside — this included cabinets, even the carpet, nails, roof material, trusses. It helped not being the contractor, just a worker looking to make a little extra money. I did extremely well and built these six houses, but of course none of them were finished and already sold another one before one is finished.

Mixed lumber normally did not sell a house in Spokane, but because I bought the six houses and delivered it. It came out very well. But my family was not really interested to move to Spokane because they lived in nice Monterey. So, I did extremely well at that time next to Monterey. It had a lot of rentals, but I had a rental in the gray house in Seaside. This man, he was almost forcing for me and almost came to me daily saying he wanted to buy the house.

I said it was fine. He got a loan on the house. I released the money to going bigger and going to another step to doing something. I sold that gray house for the person renting it when the house was new. He wanted to buy it.

Monterey had a very nice subdivision called the Peter Gate over there. I did not worry about the high-class neighbors like I did in Hungary. But back at the condominium, I always wanted to do the best for my family. Because my kids and at this time, my wife had a very high appreciation, it made me extremely happy to see my family happy. I tried to do something for my mom to make her happy. Finally, I had a dream she was going to hug me and kiss me and say, "You're so nice, Ferenc." But it did not happen.

But it's okay. I accept my mother now. Even then, it didn't matter how much had happened. I am sixty-three and a half years old now; she locked the gate, not taking out the chain. But, in my heart, I still love her even when she died. When I left Hungary, she was alive. The last time I saw her face, she was alive, and I couldn't believe she died. She is still in my heart, and I have a nice place there. I don't want to change my mind; she died and I'm not going to see her ever again. But I feel fine about that.

I bought that house in a very nice neighborhood. Of course, the house needed to be remodeled. What happened, you're not going to believe it. I had to put it in this book. One friend was a teacher who lived in a house – a single teacher. It was amazing that man was by himself with no family. But the teacher over there was using a drug, some kind of drug. I'm not going to tell you what kind of drug. It's no reason to find out. Never want to find out then but I know what had happened.

He had a house valued about around $300,000. But I wasn't not sure if he owed money for some reason he had to come up with money overnight which was $175,000. Escrow closed on the gray house, plus I had saved money and he knew I had cash.

He said, "Ferenc, you want an amazing deal and to double your money immediately?"

I said, "Of course, I know you know me. I'm interested."

I went over there and bought the house and bailed him out of it. In the next couple days, I paid the house off. But the house was in terrible shape. I took everything out and put in new carpet and made the whole bathroom new. I did everything as much as I could. Not much, but what I needed to do, so I did it. I did not make it like a new house.

He bought the gray house, he put it on a contract. But when he bought the gray, he put it over there whenever I wanted to sell the peach house where I was living that I was to let him make a deal and he would be the first buyer for that house. I was not crazy to and happy to do it on that kind of deal, but he was so nice to me. Mostly people that came like a real friend, I did not know many people like that. I had a problem that some people would turn to the point of jealousy about what I did. But only his parents or his sister were interested in buying that house.

I got the house and finished the construction. His name was Joe. I told him, "Hey, Joe, the house is for sale."

He said, "Are you serious?"

I said, "Yes, I am." I made the deal because the escrow in his loan was time concerned. I moved in a new house over there. It was on top of a hill and the reason I moved over there was not because of the ocean view. But it had a view to Monterey Bay. I said somebody later will enjoy it in some way a point to selling the house.

What had happened was the house escrow and so many things were in time constraint so he made it to rent to own or an option lease to buy. They rented. I mean everything had happened in about two or three weeks because the escrow had closed very fast, another house, and then I did the remodeling and the time went to get everything finished.

I moved in a house and he moved in on this beach house and everything just came out perfect. About four and a half months later, his escrow went through the beach house, too. I lived in a high-class neighborhood because I had a chance to go that way. Not because I wanted to do it that way, but I had a chance to do it. So, everything was great then.

And then, asI had already mentioned, this started a bit of a marriage problem.

Chapter 6

Daughter and Son

I would like to continue my story and talk about my daughter and son. I have already mentioned that my daughter was born on August 29, 1972. She was a beautiful girl. Her mom didn't have any complications with the pregnancy, and she had a normal delivery. She was not like a newborn baby but just like a week old because her mom delivered her without any complications.

For me, in my life, it was an extremely big change because I always needed time to be with my child. After four days, she came home. My wife brought her home and I gave her the first bath in the evening. Everything went so well. Day by day, I had a big change in my life, in my happiness. I let her mom stay home with her. My life, again, had completely changed.

I reorganized my time in how I was working. I always worked long hours, so, in the morning, I did not have a chance to spend time with her because I went to work very early. But I made time to go home because, as I mentioned, in Hungary, had the biggest meal at noon. After lunch, I always stayed home for about two hours. Then, I took a half hour nap with her, and she slept in my arms many times. Everything was very peaceful.

I learned how much I missed my parents' love. But I wouldn't complain about that. I accepted what my parents were able to give to me. I already mentioned it, but even that I never thought about if I always liked or loved my parents. I loved my parents and I appreciated what they did for me.

My wife and I decided to have another child soon because I wanted to raise them together with not a big age difference. For that reason, my wife delivered a second child on February 24, 1975. This was a third unbelievably happy day for me. Again, my wife didn't have any complications during her pregnancy and delivered him very easily. It took four days to bring him home.

My daughter was jumping around, and even though she was just two years old, she was extremely happy to see a newborn baby. She realized he was her brother. My wife was already home raising my daughter, and now had two beautiful children. I bought a new washing machine for her, an automatic washing machine. It was totally different than what she had before.

I was working all the time, and then I went early in the morning to work. I went home about 7:30 in the morning. I would go back and spend breakfast with my two beautiful children. I went home at noon and stayed home for two hours and took a half hour nap with my two beautiful children.

As I mentioned earlier in my book, I was very young when I thought I would go to the United States. But it was just a dream as a child. One relative's son was in United States, and another, his daughter, was in Australia. I was talking about it, which was interesting.

I think I was about nine when I said, "One day I'm going to the United States, too." But again, that was just a remark I said as a child.

At that time, it became interesting in Hungary as a communist country. I was able to leave for the United States because my mother-in-law made time to help my wife. My sister was glad to help her. I made a short trip to the United States.

I said, "Okay, I'm going to see this country and how it looks in case something doesn't work out in Hungary, because my parents defected from communism. They were innocent, but they blamed my family." I'm not going into detail since I already mentioned it before.

I went to the United States and saw it was a beautiful country. I realized, if somebody was working hard or wanted to work, there were possibilities. I talked to my relative's son and his friend and they said:

"This is a country looking for a hardworking people."

I knew I was a hardworking person.

So, I went back to Hungary. Of course, I missed my children a lot and had even more appreciation for my mother-in-law and sister for what they did for me while I was visiting the United States for a couple months. But, I was still working to stay in my country because my children had a grandma. It must be mentioned that my parents were not happy about my marriage. I had two children and, slowly, I was working hard to make contact and return to Hungary with my two children so they could meet their grandma and grandpa on the farm. That worked out because I worked very hard.

But my parents made a difference with my two children, especially my youngest brother's child. I will only mention this one thing. I don't want to go through all the sad details. I was visiting my two children on my parents' farm and my mother gave me a homemade cookie for my brother's son when he was a boy. She locked him in a room, gave him a cookie, but did not give a cookie for my sweet child.

I won't say my brother's son was not a kindhearted and loving boy to his grandparents. But again, my child received different love and attention from grandma; my youngest brother was treated differently with her son and it was sad. He was an alcoholic and had an extremely nice wife, but my brother controlled her very much.

I raised my two sweet children with love and attention. I spent time in the morning with them. I had to be to work, but I thought it was more important to spend the time in the morning and at noon with my sweet children. I stopped to work at 5:30, 5:45, and then I went home and I spent time with them from 6:00 to 8:00 P.M. until they went to bed.

My children had a special TV show they watched in Hungary from 6:00 to 6:30 P.M. I would find a book to read with my children. We would play together and many times I went back to my garage to work on engines or transmissions late. It was normal for me to go to bed at 9:30 or at the latest 10:00 P.M. Many times, I had to be to work to earn money for my family.

I had many friends who had appreciation. I had Steve. When I was a child, he gave me a lot of attention. One uncle and his wife gave me a lot of attention and, of course, Steve's wife, too. But I was amazed how much both of them – my uncle and his wife and Steve and his wife – liked my children. They took care of them like grandchildren, especially Steve, since he didn't have kids or grandkids, for some reason. I had extremely nice friends who were like family.

My son started school in the first elementary. My daughter finished the second and stepped into third elementary, and both were in the same school. They each had two different teachers, but both believed in communism. It didn't matter how young my children were. My daughter said one teacher was very mean to her and called her names. Another teaching my son was a relative and gave him a hard time.

I said, "Oh no. I'm not going to step into the same problem in a school." Many teachers gave me a hard time in school. But I didn't have a way to change anything. I didn't have a chance to say or do anything. I had to accept it.

I need to mention it now. My daughter went to third elementary. She got a cold and I took her to a doctor. She said she had to take three different shots this Friday morning, Saturday, and Sunday. On Monday, she had to check to make sure everything came out alright. We came Sunday morning from a doctor visit for the last shot.

My daughter said, "Daddy, one day I'm going to be a doctor also."

I said, "I hope so, and I'm want to help you to make it happen."

I will tell you later why I mentioned that.

My daughter loved to come to the farm. At this time, I had my own dairy farm and geese farm. She loved animals. It was sad for my son.

I need to tell a sad story. My wife showed a difference in attention towards our two children and gave more to our son. I was not a person to say she was better to our son, but one thing I had to say was she gave him more attention. She did not want him to go to the farm. She did not have to tell my daughter to go to the farm. I think she said, "Don't go with Daddy." I didn't think she would change her mind. She really wanted to go to the farm.

I did not mention that one time my daughter said, "Daddy, I'm going to sleep in your arms, and then when you wake, I'm going to wake up too because I want to go with you to the farm."

But my heart would break if I woke her up. So, what I did was I went to the farm at 3:00 A.M. and finished milking the cows. I went back to pick her up because I knew she loved to stay on the farm.

I saw that my son did not want to come with us, so I did not say anything. I just said, "Stay home, my dear, and enjoy your time with your mother." Of course, my wife did not like it and was not interested in going to the farm. In the whole year, she did not visit my farm. But I accepted it because I loved her and she delivered these two beautiful children to me, and was nice to me, too.

My wife and I had different attitudes; I accepted her when I met and got married to her in the beginning, but I changed my mind and attention to how she was doing. I accepted her for good, bad or any way. Working with, not just marriage, with any business partnership or anything, I thought everybody needed to make decisions at to what was good for another person and not try to change friends or business partners or anything when it came to attitude or mindset. I had to accept it if I wanted to continue the friendship or partnership. But, in my marriage, I accepted it and loved what she did or liked it. I got a flower for her to try to make her happy.

I did not buy a lot of toys for my children, but I bought some. I did not pile the toys. I just bought what was necessary but made more time to with play with different things. I liked to play together, or read a book, or go to the backyard and play in the sand, and so many other things together. But it did not mean I was buying one toy that was good for two days and on the third day buying another one. Not because I couldn't afford it. I just did not think it was necessary to buy a bunch of toys to make them happy for a couple days. I told them what they needed to learn to play with one day for one way and another day for another way. So, just a little on that, but day by day just came extremely easily.

I would never forget when my daughter was in fourth elementary and she came to my farm. One man was not doing his job well.

My daughter said, "Daddy, look at him. He's taking care of the cows and not doing his job very well." She said, "Please tell this guy to be patient with the poor cows and don't be mean to them." She's a very interesting person.

My son, he's a very interesting, but totally different than my daughter. But I have never, ever been favorable to one over the other. Both of them were the sweetest people to me, equally. I had not opened my mind to which one was nicer, which one was better; to me, my daughter had always called my name, and I accepted it how it was growing up with my son. I did not insist his mother give more attention to our daughter or to keep close to our son because maybe they would have a problem later for that.

My daughter he was in fourth elementary, as I mentioned, as to how it was to work on the farm and my son was in second elementary. The teacher really made a hard time for my child. There were a number of things that made me think about leaving Hungary.

My mother was unhappy, since my farm was growing very fast and big. She did not like it because I did not follow her rules. She said, "Don't make my farm bigger." It was in my blood because I had that from my grandpa. My great grandpa, actually, and then I did it. My grandpa too, but somebody said I was similar to my great grandpa.

So many things happened and I decided to immigrate to the United States on August 17, 1983. I planned it and worked very hard to make sure everything was working very well. I didn't want to hurt my children and wife, and I didn't want any damage for the whole family to leave a beautiful country.

It was very painful for me. It hurt a lot of friends – my uncle and his wife, Steve and his wife, and, of course, my mother-in-law. I know it deeply hurt her not see her beautiful grandkids. But, to me, I didn't have another choice because I was unable to get to the next step in Hungary. Even if I needed to do something or fight against these many problems, I didn't want to say anything to damage my two beautiful children. For that reason, I decided to leave Hungary.

So, I made it happen. I went through the Austria border and then after I crossed the border, I stopped. As I mentioned it, I brought my children's favorite dog. Some guy stopped the car and I told the kids what had happened. My son realized what I was talking about, but especially my daughter, because she was fourteen years old.

For some reason, she made a lot of attention for that dog. She held that dog and started to cry.

Her mother said, "Why are you crying? Are you sorry for grandma?"

She said, "No, no, no. I have a favorite cow and his name is Mafla. I miss her a lot."

I said, "Well, she's too big to bring, too." I needed to make it the next day because the family went around midnight – eleven to midnight – to the Hungarian and Austrian border.

The next day I stepped in the immigration office to apply to immigrate to the United States. In Austria, I got a very nice place at a motel to stay with my family. For the next couple days, I got a job over there to make a little money. Not much, but I made a little money because I mostly got everything. I was unable to have extra shirts and pants for my children.

I did not say if I go to the UN office and not getting something for the kids. I always liked to work and earn money because a lot of other people were unable since they didn't have the skill to make extra money. It was better to leave what they had in the UN office for those kids.

The time came on December 19, 1983 for the whole family to go to the United States. I would never forget the UN at the airport made a picture for the family and I needed to hold the dog in my hands. I brought my dog to the United States, too. I mentioned bringing my dog was more complicated because I spent – for quarantine, a cage and a shot – almost $1000 or closer to $967.

We went to the airport and flew to the United States. First, the plan was to go to the Kennedy airport in New York. And here was something a bit interesting. My nephew was in New York. We were supposed to be going to his apartment. I landed in Kennedy airport around 4:00 P.M., and he left to Hungary at 8:00 P.M. So, really, we spent time together for about two and a half hours.

 niece lived in Astoria, New York. She got a home for my family at my nephew's apartment. So, the apartment was just so interesting and nice. But not just his apartment but every apartment had a lot of cockroaches. He was single and it was not really a beautiful apartment. But I was not worried about that because I knew it was temporary. But the biggest problem was my daughter and son were scared of the cockroaches and afraid to go to in the bathroom and so many things.

My wife's cousin lived in north California, Redding. They continued to make something happen even though I got job. I had another option to work with another person because I specialized in Mercedes and German cars – BMW and Volkswagen. I did not take into consideration how much money or what was good for me. I followed what my wife wanted. I said, "Okay, if your cousin can help us to go to California, go ahead and do it," even though I had already a job. I had Social Security. I immediately had a friend.

On January 15, 1984 we flew to the Oakland, California airport. Over there my wife's cousin was waiting for us along with her husband and his two children. They had a minivan and it had room for everybody. They took everybody home with just everything – just sit, go inside and were extremely nice to us. I remember I met her before she immigrated to the United States. I met her in Hungary two times briefly. I remembered her a bit. She remembered me a bit. But everything came out so nice.

We flew over there, I think, on a Tuesday actually. Not this week, the following week, I had a place for my daughter and my son to go to school. And here is just a bit about my job. I did not get paid very well for my job in a wrecking yard. I figured out that the money was not enough to raise a family over there with renting a place and then, as I just mentioned, I was almost ready to go back to New York.

I met somebody in New York. She didn't want me to go back to New York. She said, "I have a brother who is a Catholic priest down in Monterey. Why don't you just go?" This lady, I met in New York. She and her brother stepped in my life. I got the ticket to go down to Monterey. It didn't matter how much it broke my heart, I went down to Monterey to look at it what was possible and I saw that I had big opportunities to work in Monterey and then raise my family over there.

Monterey had more Hungarian people and then they were able to help me a lot because I didn't speak English. I had a chance to work at Star Motor to rebuild engines over there with a contract, not hourly, and I didn't need to speak with anybody. A lot of Hungarian people wanted to me paint their houses and then I knew well how I needed to paint the houses.

I decided to stay in Monterey. I stayed away from my family and really it was hard for me. One way is about 320 miles so back and forth, it's 640 miles. I had to make it because I could not handle not seeing my family on the weekends. I drove over there on a Saturday evening and I would be back sometime Sunday evening or early Monday morning to work and make money.

I worked as fast as I could to make a house in Monterey for a family. This time I had a Hungarian friend. His name was Steve and his stepson's friend had a Volkswagen Vanagon. I got this Volkswagen Vanagon for free, but it had a problem with the engine. I got this car and Steve helped me to replace the engine so I would have a car.

Also, another Hungarian family's mother died and had an Oldsmobile Delta 88. I got that for free. That car really did not need a lot work just because it was sitting in a garage for many years. It just needed for me to make it happen to run again and the registration. So, everything came out okay.

It did not immediately at first. I fixed the Volkswagen Vanagon. I was working hard to make a house ready to go to for my family. I finished that and I went up to northern California and about April 1984, I brought my family to the beautiful city of Monterey. Over there had a school that had a lot of people from around the world. The children going to this special school didn't speak a lot of English.

I never mentioned it, but when my daughter was already in Hungary, she learned some English in class. I didn't pay a school. I just hired a private teacher. But my son was too young for that. They went to this special program and also a lot of other Hungarian families had kids and helped to do so many things for my children. So, everything just went nicely. I was so happy because the family was together again and everything.

My son and my daughter both stepped back one year in school to see how to start working on it. My daughter went back to a normal year in school after almost a couple months, and my son took a special test at the end of the year and went back to a normal year of school. But my son, for some reason, was a very shy person because he always wanted to stay next to his mommy. He had a harder time than my daughter on mostly everything. But both of them were extremely intelligent kids at school and everything worked very well. My daughter and my son delivered the newspaper. The reason I wanted them to deliver the newspaper was, not for me, but to teach my children how to make money and have an independent life. They did it in morning.

I met many people, including one family from Pakistan. It was a place called Fisherman's Wharf in Monterey and he had a famous restaurant called Fisherman's Grotto. In the front of Fisherman's Grotto, they were selling flowers over there. And then we changed it. My son and daughter were selling flowers for a couple hours to make a little money.

My son went to help after fifth grade at an animal shelter to take care of dogs, cats, and birds. But my daughter, when she was in seventh grade, went to many nursing homes to help old people. When she was at the nursing home, she got a job. She did volunteer work and then finished eighth grade and started high school. She had a chance to work two hours a day, four days a week to make money in a nursing home. She also did volunteer work at the Knights of Columbus. It was the same thing — helping old people. Everything went well for my children, and I was so happy.

I was happy because I had a job and a lot of people liked my work. I had a chance to remodel and paint houses and work on cars. Mostly, I specialized in rebuilding engines and transmissions because I did not need to do it. I would finish a job overnight. So, in everything, I was so happy to do it.

My daughter, of course, continued her studies to go to a medical school. After she finished high school, she went to college at UCLA. She did extremely well there and started living in a dorm. But the dorm was very crowded and noisy for her. After a half year, I helped her move into a private house with another girl.

In the private house, the rent was very expensive in Santa Monica, Los Angeles, California. Because her room was so small, I mentioned to her I wouldn't mind building a loft in that room. So, I did. She talked to her landlord and then the next weekend I went over there and met the landlord. He let me build a loft. I used a beautiful cedar and redwood material to build a nice loft. Her roommate used the upstairs loft. Even her desk was in a room upstairs because it had a very high ceiling and my daughter's bed and desk was downstairs. It had a nice balcony, and it all came out nicely.

Los Angeles to Monterey was not too far. It was about 180 miles one way to visit her. Mostly, she came to see me. I went down to pick her up on Friday evening and then I took her back on Sunday evening, or she came home on the weekend. When I did go down to Los Angeles, I was always using a house kitchen or sometimes if her roommate was busy and did not want to do it, I rented a motel that had a kitchen and made homemade food for my daughter. She was so happy.

I want to step back to my son. He had a lovely friend in school; He was just a beautiful person with a great personality. He finished eighth grade and stepped in high school in Monterey. He finished high school in Monterey and decided attend a firefighting school and everything went very well for them. But he was still extremely close to his mom and that made things harder for them. But I never wanted to change her mind.

I said, "Do it the way you like to do it." I accepted it and I tried to hope for the best.

Chapter 7

Daughter

Then Annamaria finished her degree at UCLA. Of course, she applied to medical schools. She was not accepted to any of the schools she applied. As everyone knows, it's not easy to be accepted into medical school. So, she spent the summer at home. Even though she grew older, she and I never fought. I tried to tell her about what I thought she should do. But she would watch her mother and I and liked what we did. Before I would say, "Do it," she had already done it. I was always amazed at how hard she worked and what a nice daughter she was.

Then, Annamaria decided to go to Ann Arbor, Michigan for graduate school to study public health because she could not get into a med school. She said, "Daddy, you don't mind taking me to Ann Arbor, Michigan?"

I said, "Of course, I'll do it!"

She flew to Ann Arbor to check out where she would be going to go to school and started the paperwork. Then she found a place — not a dorm, of course, but in a private house. Then she came back. Before she started the semester in Ann Arbor, she and I drove there. It took two or three days. It was a long drive. I did my best for her over there to make sure her room was comfortable. The next spring, her mother went to visit her. Ann Arbor is a beautiful city. Of course, she always flew home as much as she could to spend time at home during the breaks. Everything was going so amazingly well in life.

The next year after spring break, Annamaria went back to Ann Arbor. Then her mother and I drove there. My niece lived in New York City, so I said, "Why not just drive to New York City? Then I'll show you and my wife Manhattan."

I had been to Manhattan four or five times because of my niece and nephew. We drove to Long Island, New York and spent four or five days there. Then we went to New York City then back to Ann Arbor.

When Annamaria finished the first year, I went to Ann Arbor to bring her home. I was amazed again at how she had set up her summer work. She was working that summer in northern California in the Public Health Department. Whenever she flew home, she would make a friend. She would tell us, "He's a professor. He's this or that." Then she went back to school for her second year in public health. That fall, I didn't visit her, but I did in the spring. Then I went to New York to visit my niece and to do a little work there and make a little money. Then I came home.

Annamaria finished school and I brought her home. I'll never forget. I went there with an empty car to bring her stuff home and she kept saying:

"One more thing, one more thing, one more thing."

I kept reorganizing the car to fit one more thing, one more thing. So, finally, we finished putting everything in the car.

After we finished, she had me go to the supermarket to buy some food. Annamaria and I loved French bread. The supermarket had some recently taken out of the oven, hot French bread. I bought some and butter and meat. I think she loved it, and I liked it very much. I had cheese and milk. I finished the shopping and tried to put the groceries in the car.

Then I told my daughter, "I'm sorry, my dear, believe it or not, I don't have room to put it in the car. You have to put it next to your feet or someplace because I can't put these two loaves of bread in the car." She and I have mentioned it many times and never forgotten how much stuff she had from her college room. We didn't even have room for two loaves of French bread!

We had an amazing time. I always loved to go down to UCLA, and then Ann Arbor because I knew I'd be talking to my daughter for the next three days because it was a long drive to get home.

We made it to California, and Annamaria was working hard to get into medical school, and still she didn't have a chance. She got a very good job in public health and moved to Sacramento. I helped as much as I could to make her place comfortable, and then I got her a beautiful BMW, and she was so happy. It was nice for me, because she would drive home, and everything was going so well.

It didn't matter how nice the people she met at work were, her dream was to go to medical school. She earned some money and found the best option to get accepted to medical school. She worked for a year and a half. Then she said, "Daddy, I'd like to move to San Francisco to do a fifteen-month special course to get into medical school."

I said, "Well, okay. You know I'd go with you any place in the world and I'd help you as much as I could to find a very nice place."

You know, of course I had gone to Sacramento with her and did to improve her room and kitchen to make the place nice for her. It was a hundred degrees Fahrenheit in northern California, Redding and it didn't go well in San Francisco with a short tent. It was fifty-five in San Francisco for the spring break. I'll never forget the road over there. Everything went so well on 12th Street. She and I had a beautiful time. Because Annamaria had an extremely sweet personality, she always changed the atmosphere into a friendly one in every house. She had the best personality. She was able to study and continued to the next step of what was in her mind and her dream.

Annamaria finished the fifteen-month program or was supposed to finish it. She said, "Daddy, I made out an application to New York and Davis in California." Also, a couple of other places like Ann Arbor, Michigan and Utica, New York. Then she said, "Daddy, I'm going to an interview in New York."

In 1988 or 1989, I had visited Utica, New York. It's a beautiful place. I visited the medical school and heard they had a great medical school. So, she applied there.

Annamaria went by plane to New York and by train to Utica. I'll never forget, she said, "Everything went well." On her way back to New York to the airport, the train, she mentioned she needed to go to the bathroom. She left her briefcase and stuff on a seat and asked somebody, "Please watch my stuff over there because I need to go to the bathroom." She came out and the person had left. But she was lucky because there was a man and wife nearby who had watched her stuff.

The man asked, "Where did you come from, sweetie?"

She said, "Well, I came from California."

Then he asked, "And what did you do here?"

She said, "I interviewed at a medical school because I'd like to go to medical school."

The man said, "Do you know who I am?"

My daughter said, "No, I don't know who you are. It's the first time I've seen you."

He said, "Well, I am a professor at that school."

That man became her friend. But that was not the only time. She always met very nice people, or the right people; the ones she needed to find.

I'll never forget one time, Annamaria told me, "Daddy, I'm going to fly to northern California or Los Angeles." She spoke to somebody on the plane and then asked, "Then what did you do?"

The man was in the medical field. He said, "You know what? You're so sweet and it's so nice to talk to you. Can I take you home? My wife is coming to pick me up and I'd like for you to come to dinner."

This didn't happen one time, but many times. She would meet the right person she needed to find because she was an extremely special person. She always knew what she needed to do next to make her dream come true.

Of course, Annamaria got the chance to go to medical school in New York. But she was so smart and did a lot at UC Davis in California. Of course, UC Davis was cheaper and closer to our family, so, she decided to stay in California and start medical school at UC Davis. It was her dream, my dream, and the family's dream. Annamaria started medical school.

I'm telling you, I couldn't believe it. Even though I was her father, it was hard to believe it, and hard to see how much capability this one woman had. I'm not saying she's taken my game, but if I want to do something, I don't look at what's hard to do. I look at what's the best thing to do. I saw that she was the same way.

Annamaria would say, "I'm going to do it!" And she did it.

When she went to Davis, she lived in a very nice apartment. Of course, I went to visit her many times. But she would usually come home because she liked homemade food. It was always Mommy's homemade food. I liked to do so many things, but I was so busy working to pay bills. My wife was a good cook, and my daughter loved to eat Mommy's food every day, and this was normal.

One day, Anna said, "Daddy, guess what? I met a boy in the library."

I said, "Okay, it's time, my dear, for you to find somebody because, someday, I'm going to need grandchildren. But I know you can't do that immediately because first you want to finish medical school."

One day, I went to her place and this boy she had met had already left. My chocolate puppy – was about ten weeks old at the time – and I'll never forget, my puppy wanted to pee and play on the grass. I saw a boy who was at least six-foot-five walking and took a look over. Believe it or not, my little puppy stopped and looked at him.

I told my puppy, "I hope this is the boy who my daughter met because it seems to me he is a very nice man." Of course, I was just telling my puppy because nobody was there.

He left, and I went up to Annamaria's apartment. I said, "My dear, I saw one boy who was at least six-foot-five. I hope he is your boyfriend."

"Daddy, yes he is," she said.

I said, "Okay, because my puppy is happy, too. He was so anxious to see this nice person."

Annamaria was just so happy.

To go back a little, my daughter liked to travel by airplane. She went to Chicago and Sweden for a seminar. She asked me one time, "Daddy, what do you think if I go there?"

I said, "Of course, go ahead! You don't have to stay at home and sit. You can go anywhere. You always learn more. The more you see new things in the world, the more you know the best way and what is not very good and what is very nice. Just always be very careful, because it's not hard to find strangers in the world. You'd better be careful. Go with somebody before you say something or do something." Even if I hadn't mentioned it to her, she thought in that way. Her ideas and mine were always similar.

Her medical studies were going very well. I couldn't believe it. I'd see her studying all her books. I was amazed. She worked hard and she had a very nice apartment.

Then, one day, she said, "What do you think, Daddy? My boyfriend, Mark, and I decided to rent a place together." They decided they were going to get married.

I said, "Well, my dear, I do think about that. You know I never push you or tell you to do it, but I have already thought it is probably better for both of you to live together in one place and do things together."

For some reason, I never had very much money to give Annamaria for a big wedding. I did as much as I could. My future son-in-law's parents came up with the money and they had a very nice wedding. I can't tell you, it was like I had a dream to have a child, and got the child, this special, special person – to go step by step, following my dream.

I told her, "Well, I hope your dream was to find this nice boy, and that this boy's dream was also to find you; I have a feeling your dream and his dream are coming true." This nice man had the money to have a nice wedding.

I was always so happy I had gotten married, and that my daughter and son were born. Every day, it made me happy and kept me on top of the water. I always saw in front of me a big hill. I would say, "Okay, I need to climb up to the top of this big hill." You know when everything is going well, there's always something that stops or gives you a hard time to get to the next step. But because I had an extremely nice daughter and son, they helped me to see how amazing my daughter was and how amazing what she was doing.

I'll never forget. I bought a suit for her wedding and I stopped at this store I used to go to and the clerk said:

"Frank, I've never seen you dressed this nice! You look like you're ten or fifteen years younger! What has happened to you? Did you get a new car or what? Did you win the lottery or what? Why are you so happy?"

"Oh," I said, "if I won the lottery and had a million dollars, I'd never dream of a new car. You know what's happening tomorrow?" I said, "You don't know what is happening!"

She said, "What, what? Tell me!"

I said, "Okay, I'll tell you. My daughter's wedding is tomorrow."

She said, "Oh, my God! I didn't know." She saw me often in the store, but I never told her I had a nice daughter and son. Then one day, she saw something different. I wasn't dressed in work clothes. I was dressed in a nice suit. I looked so happy. I looked ten or fifteen years younger. I had a nice haircut and everything. She thought, "Definitely, there's a big change in this man!"

Then, I'll never forget, we drove to San Francisco, and we stayed in a motel. I was walking around at the motel and my daughter called me.

She said, "Daddy, is everything fine?"

I said, "Everything is fine. Yes, everything is good."

Even in a motel, actually, in the lobby, a clerk said, "Man, you're having a very special day. You're dressed nice and you look so happy."

I said, "Of course, my daughter's wedding is tomorrow!"

He asked, "Where is your daughter's wedding?"

I told him, "Not too far from here. In that one old church built in the 18th century."

He said, "Yes, I think I know that place!"

The next morning, I woke up and went to pick up my daughter. My car was always running fine though it was not a new car. I went to Davis to pick her up to take her to her wedding, and guess what? I was coming out from her apartment and the car wouldn't start.

My daughter said, "Daddy, don't worry about it."

I said, "I can't tell you how happy I am. But one thing, you're not going to make this wedding."

She said, "No, no." She immediately called a tow truck company. Somebody gave us a jumpstart and we made it to an auto parts store and replaced the battery. Then everything went well and we made it to her wedding. But I'll tell you one thing, every time I get close to San Francisco place it's just terrible. All the places were mostly foggy or cold.

But everyone wanted to listen to her wedding; even the wind stopped and wasn't making any noise; the leaves listened to the pastor. It was at a high elevation and you could look out the windows.

I said, "Look, even the ocean doesn't have waves!" The ocean was quiet! It didn't want to make any noise. Everyone was listening to what the pastor was saying and what my daughter and her future husband were saying. Then my daughter turned to him and he turned to her and there was the most beautiful sunshine and the bluest sky I'd ever seen in my life. It was so bright; I'd never seen in my whole life. Everybody there was smiling and everything was just beautiful.

When I was walking around, I said, "It seems like I'm not even walking on the floor! I'm floating!" I went into the lobby. My daughter and son-in-law had prepared a table with my country's flag, and there was a basket with paprika. I said, "It's okay." That guy was just amazing.

Oh my God, the ceremony inside the church because she and he were so beautiful! Everyone was so quiet. I saw everybody watching her and then looking at me. It was not the first time my son-in-law's relatives had seen me. I couldn't hide how happy I was. I had the feeling I had been born again! I was in a different world.

Then we went inside for dinner. It was a special day for everyone. Everyone took a look inside the room to see so many happy people to see these people's dream come true. I thanked my son-in-law's parents for putting on this amazing, special ceremony.

I tried making a little speech about how happy I was. I didn't hide it. It didn't matter how happy I was, I had a hard time saying what a special person my daughter was, and how happy I was she had such a special man for her husband. The wedding went so well. I was just amazed.

Then Annamaria and my son-in-law found a special place to move. They worked hard. My daughter was going to school and working hard. I thank God I was able to replace her BMW with a nice Mercedes. I couldn't tell you how long I waited for her to finish medical school. I knew when she finished, she and her husband immediately wanted a baby. Thank God my daughter and son-in-law read my mind, and they always did everything in the best way.

I'll never forget, my daughter called me and said, "Daddy, I have news for you."

I said, "I have a feeling what you're going to say but go ahead and tell me before I say it. I know you want to tell me." I didn't say, "You're pregnant with your first baby." I wanted her to say it.

She heard my extremely happy voice, and, of course, she told me.

I said, "Oh my god! You don't know how happy I am to hear that."

Everything went so well, because she was pregnant and stayed in school. She was working hard, of course, and my son-in-law and she decided to go to school and to work. I thought of my son-in-law there, and my daughter got some extra work and finished medical school. Finally, after so many years of hard work, I was just amazed. I couldn't believe how hard Annamaria worked; she never wanted to waste time. She finished her degree in public health and she worked in the public health field, and everybody liked her a lot and were amazed at how smart she was. Because of her dream, she took the step to go to medical school. I saw how hard my child worked. At ten o'clock, eleven, midnight, she was still studying. And she did it. Her dream came true.

Then she got a paper. She finished medical school and said, "Well, Daddy, I'm going to deliver a baby, but I still have a long way to go to start working as a doctor." She had to do an internship, which she did at Sacramento Hospital. Of course, I helped as much as I could. I didn't stop following my dream to help her. One day, she said, "Daddy, I am pregnant with a girl."

I said, "You know what I think. It doesn't matter if it's a boy or a girl, but you know how I have my heart set on it being a girl. It doesn't matter if it's a girl or a boy, but this way, it's a complete family."

She and her husband were working hard, and on October 28, she delivered a girl. You wouldn't believe, but she delivered a baby girl in the hospital and I was her first caller. A couple of minutes after she delivered her baby, I called. I had that much feeling in my heart and mind for her. Everything went fine. She delivered a beautiful, sweet, baby girl. Everything went well without any complications and she was taken home.

Of course, her husband, Mark, was there, too, from the start of the delivery. I went there to visit Annamaria. My daughter and son-in-law were both in bed holding the baby. It was so cute. I was amazed at what a nice way it was to start to raise this baby. Everything went well, and my daughter was taken home. I couldn't tell you guys how nice it was, and how much power was given to me to help her to the next step to finish her internship.

My daughter and son-in-law moved from their apartment into a three-bedroom house. It was a more peaceful and quiet place to raise a kid. I was amazed at my daughter. She was doing her internship, and my son-in-law was still working, too. He was also still working to finish his doctorate. Both were also still working, of course, to pay the bills. I was amazed at how organized they were. Many times, I was at their house, and I saw how they would wait till my granddaughter went to sleep. Then my daughter and son-in-law would sit down and talk about their plans for the next day. They worked really well together.

I went to New York, where my niece lived, to work there. But my daughter and I had a daily connection. She wanted to let me know everything that was going on there.

Then, one day my daughter called me and said, "Apa." Apa means *Daddy* in Hungarian. "Guess what? What would you think if I had another baby?"

I said, "Well, how old are you? You're not a teenager. You're getting close to your forties. You'd better do it soon. At this time, I think two kids born in a short time and growing up together is much better at your age."

You see, my wife delivered two babies in a short time, because I said, "It's better not to have a big age difference between children." I always liked the idea of having three kids, but my wife was not interested in going through another pregnancy. I knew my daughter was trying to tell me something.

Then she said, "Daddy, you know, I'm probably pregnant."

Then I said, "I hope so! Because, again, you'd better be having another baby soon."

Then about a month and a half later, she told me she was checking to see how the baby was doing and if it was a boy or a girl. You're not going to believe it, but because I was a twin, I was already holding my breath. I said, "I hope she'll tell me some beautiful news." And guess what?

She told me, "Daddy, guess what? I am pregnant with twins!"

I was almost unable to speak. I had had so much happiness in my life. She and my son were born. You know, every kid is different, and some fight about doing their homework, and some need punishment. But she was— not because she was my daughter, but even if I knew her or she was my neighbor — she did so well. I would definitely have said, "She is definitely a very special person."

Because I was a twin, I felt like I was born again, or that I had stepped into a different world. Any time I heard my daughter's or son-in-law's voices, I felt tingling along my spine. I had a wonderful feeling, and said, "Thank God! I know they would do an amazing job!"

Then it came time for her to deliver the twins. It was the beautiful month of May – May 13th, and she delivered two healthy boys. Of course, my daughter worked almost till the last minute. She was doing her internship at the hospital. I came back to California and tried to help as much as I could to help raise my sweet granddaughter. She came to look at the twin boys. I saw how happy my granddaughter was to see her new brother. I saw happiness on my sweet granddaughter's face.

Of course, I was always telling my daughter and son-in-law, "Well, guys, I know Annamaria has to go to work after six weeks; and I know Mark has to go to work. I know this is not a piece of cake, and not much fun, but I'll help as much as I can. I know everyone will also help you to get through this hard work. But these children will grow up together, and it will be much easier to raise children and enjoy life."

Of course, my daughter and son-in-law were always organized, and had a plan for how they would raise these three children.

They stayed in their private, three-bedroom house. My son-in-law was a professor, and my daughter was almost a doctor. It was amazing how organized they were. They didn't live in a mansion, but their house was nice and very clean and in a quiet, peaceful neighborhood. So, everything was going well. My son-in-law's parents lived in Alaska, and I was amazed at how often they would come to visit Mark and Annamaria and the grandkids. They were a big, big help financially and emotionally, all the time.

Of course, I had seen them many times when they came from Alaska. It wasn't possible to jump in the car and visit the kids and grandkids. It took a long time to get to them — a full day to change planes, rent a car, and such things. They came many, many times. I couldn't say how nice it was to see how happy my son-in-law's parents were. Of course, I was amazed, even my son-in-law's sister came to visit, and not just one time. I was so happy to see this great family.

Then one day, my daughter said, "Well, we may be moving someplace."

I said, "Where are you moving?"

She said, "Well, Mark is thinking about a couple different places. Maybe Michigan." She mentioned a couple different states.

I said, "Well, I know Michigan is nice, and it's not that expensive. I know you went to school for two years in Michigan." I helped her to move and visited her there. I saw what a nice place it was, and affordable.

So, my son-in-law went to an interview for a job. And then one day, my daughter and son-in-law said, "Guess what, Daddy? You know we've been thinking about moving."

I said, "I know." They had mentioned Michigan, and I think they had mentioned Maine. There was a job in California, too. I knew he had a very good job, and my daughter was so happy at Sacramento Hospital. I said, "Tell me."

She said, "We may be going to Alaska."

I said, "What are you talking about? You want to go to Alaska? Are you serious?"

She said, "Yes."

Mark's parents had a house there, and they were so nice. I couldn't tell you what a big help his parents were, and his whole family. But they didn't just help my daughter and son-in-law. I knew Mark had a brother and sister, and their parents worked very hard and also helped whichever of their children needed help. These days, one child needed help, and then another time, another child needed help. Mark's parents were well-organized in finding out which of their children needed attention. Just straight up. I was just amazed.

Then I said, "I don't know if I want you to go to Alaska or not, but, you guys, you say yes. You know that I don't care." I had gone to many states, but never Alaska.

I remember my father said, "Well, my son, Frank, is going to Alaska. He's going to survive over there, too, on top of the ice. He's not afraid of working anywhere."

Then the days went by, and my daughter said, "Are you serious? You don't mind us going to Alaska?"

I said, "Of course not, my daughter, I told you I would go anywhere to help you and my son-in-law, even if I don't say it. I have very sweet and beautiful grandkids."

Then Annamaria and Mark said, "You don't mind going there at least a month earlier to get the house ready for us to move in? The house needs a little painting and a little work, and you know how to do it."

I said, "What are you talking about? The house, sweetie? Of course, I'll do it. I'll fly over there like a bird to help you with that, to make a nice place over there for your beautiful family."

So, I had a car and a trailer, and I put in one thing and then another thing. Then I reorganized it because I wanted to bring as much as I could.

I remembered the time I went to help Annamaria move back home from Michigan, and she said, "Daddy, one more thing, and one more thing," till we didn't even have room for two loaves of bread.

Then I kept putting things into the trailer, till I said, "Oh, my God, this trailer is stacked so high!" I said, "Well, I'll just take as much as I can to Alaska." The load got higher and heavier. The only thing I could do was to drive more slowly and to be careful, and I would make it.

Of course, God was helping me. I say "God" because I believe in God, and I built my life, and God gave me everything. I just use that name, "God," and then I believe it. That's something that gives me power to do so many things. I'm not saying that someone who does not use God's name or doesn't believe in God is a bad person. Everybody chooses their own life.

Annamaria and Mark did not have time to go to church and did not talk too much about God, but I knew God was watching them and their beautiful family and giving them attention.

This family was just amazing in how beautiful and honest their lives were. They didn't talk about God, but my daughter had gotten a great education in public health because she wanted to help people. She told me, "Daddy, it's my dream to be a doctor." I knew she was not thinking about the money. She thought about how much she would be able to help people in the ways in which they needed help.

It was obvious if someone chose to become a doctor, it wasn't a piece of cake. It was very hard to get started, and you had to renew your license every ten years. Doctors didn't just fall from the sky; it took hard work. I thought everybody knew that. They had to give up a lot of freedom. She had twin boys and a girl – three kids – and did an internship. She had to work afternoons and, sometimes, the whole week. She only saw her babies, her own children, when they were sleeping. But my son-in-law did a beautiful job. It was amazing. But, as I said, my son-in-law's dream came true, as did my daughter's. Both were working hard to get what they deserved. My son-in-law deserved it, and, in the same way, so did my daughter.

A couple days before the first of June, I left California and drove through Oregon and Washington State. My son-in-law did a beautiful job marking the map in red to show how I needed to go.

He said, "Just follow this red line, and you're going to make it to Alaska." So, I drove as much as I could, and I got to the Canadian border. The border officer, seeing my happy face, must have thought: "What are you so happy about?" He actually said, "Are you going to stay in Canada, or are you going to Alaska?"

I said, "What are you talking about? Do you see this big trailer behind me? Of course, I'm going to Alaska! I'm going there to help my daughter. She's moving to Alaska."

So, I drove through Canada, and I saw many beautiful places and things. I had never been on that road before – the Alaska Highway. I was not that tired because I was always thinking, *Okay, I'll be there in three more days...two more days...one more day...in half a day.*

As I was driving through Canada, I saw moose and bears. Everything was so nice. I couldn't say how nice it was to drive through Canada. Canada was a beautiful country.

Then, finally, I got to the Alaska border and the border patrol came said, "Welcome to Alaska."

I said, "Oh, thank God, I made it! I know you're wondering why I'm so happy. I need to tell you my daughter and son-in-law and three grandkids decided to move to Alaska. I thank God I've come back on US soil, and pretty soon, I'll be in Anchorage."

So, I kept driving. In many areas, there was no phone line, but everything went well because I had a plan. I got there around noon, and it was nice and sunny. Of course, no one told me the sun wouldn't go down till 11:00 P.M. I stopped at my son-in-law's parents' house first.

They were waiting for me to have lunch. We had lunch and I told them how happy I was I had made it. My son-in-law's father took me to my children's house, and I had a surprise. That house was in one of the nicest neighborhoods. Anchorage was so great, but that neighborhood was amazing. It was a huge house. I saw what needed work, and said, "Oh, no problem. For me, it's a piece of cake."

Believe it or not, I had driven for five and a half days, and didn't hesitate to look at the house. I started working on the house at 2:30 or 3:00 that day. I started to clean, and my daughter's father-in-law showed me what he wanted to have done, approximately. I immediately saw— because I knew very well about remodeling houses —I had a lot to do. I figured out it would take one month. It was around June 3rd or 4th. I knew I would need to work very hard, and I would have to reorganize my time because the days were just flying by.

So, I started work around 3:00, and around 8:00 I saw it was not getting any darker. At 10:00, there was still sunshine. Finally, at 11:00, I said, "Well, it looks like it's getting darker." But, I wasn't tired, and I just kept working. Then I said, "Frank, you're not a robot. You need to do something to relax." I had a bed there, so I lay down and tried to sleep. Even though I had driven close to 3,000 miles, I wasn't tired because I had been thinking about how I would do the remodeling. What I would do next. How I would make this place beautiful. I was still working on it in my mind how I would do the work fast.

Then around 3:30 A.M., I went to sleep for a little while. I opened my eyes, and it was already light out, and I said, "Oh, my God, Frank, it's probably already noon! Oh, hurry, there's a lot of work to do here, and still you're sleeping!" Then I found out it was only around 4:00 in the morning. For some reason, no one told me there was such a short night there in June.

Then I started working, and I worked till it was evening. I kept working and working. Believe it or not, because of the time zone change, I didn't sleep for about four or five days. I worked day and night. Next door to that house, there was a nice neighbor lady, and later, she told me she had been watching me and asked herself:

"Where did he come from, this robot man? He's working in the early morning, and the lights are on. Then it's getting dark, and I hear the saws." I was trying not make much noise, but it wasn't hard to figure out if someone was working day and night. So, she came over and asked me, "Is everything okay? Are you doing okay?"

So, I told her, "Well, I came from California, and my daughter and her whole family are going to move here."

She said, "Oh, really? You're not tired? I saw you've — you're not bothering me — but you've been working around the clock."

I said, "I don't know what is wrong with me. I'm not able to sleep."

My daughter was calling me two or three times a day, and I would say, "Well, my dear, I'm so happy, I'm not tired. One thing I'm doing, I'm eating a lot because I'm working very hard, but I'm going to try to not drink coffee because I just can't sleep. I'm just working around the clock."

I'll never forget, after about four or five days, around 2:00 in the morning, somebody slowed down their car and stopped outside, and this guy called out. It was Mark's brother.

He said, "I don't know what you're doing to the house, but the lights are on and it looks like there's something going on. Okay, no, no, probably, my brother...I don't know...he's working." He knew it was me in the house working. He returned the next day, and said, "I know you want to finish this house, and you're being quiet, but don't kill yourself. One day, someone called and said you were working at two in the morning. I leave here in the evening and come back the next morning, and I see you've worked all night again. I'm going to turn it down because you have to go to bed and relax."

So, then, I was really working hard and I said, "Frank, you need to do a good job, and you're not going to kill yourself. Just please know you need to sleep even if the sun is not going down and how you need more sleep even if the sun comes up." Thank God, I made it.

I was working, and my daughter said, multiple times, "Daddy, it seems like you're so happy. For a long time, I haven't heard you sound this happy. What is going on?"

I said, "Are you asking me that question, my dear? I'm so happy I'm making the house beautiful. The house is big and nice and beautiful, and the neighborhood is very nice."

Everything went well, and Mark's parents came up with the money for everything. If I needed anything from Home Depot or Lowe's or any other place, there was never any fight.

He would just say, "Okay, go ahead and do it."

I remodeled, so there was a new bathroom, a new tile floor, I repaired the kitchen, painted the house, put in a new hardwood floor, took out all the carpeting and put in new carpeting, and remodeled much of the house. So, I made this house like new. One month went by fast.

My daughter and the whole family came on July 14th. I went to the airport to see my three beautiful grandkids, my daughter, and my son-in-law. Then I saw my daughter's eyes. She couldn't wait to see the house. First, I asked if everything went well the first time flying with the three grandkids, and everything had gone well. Then we went to the house, and when they went in the door, and I saw my daughter's eyes and face light up because the house was beautiful.

I couldn't believe how my son-in-law's parents were able to handle this big expense. Financially, they had to tell the tenants to move out, and there were at least a couple months with no rent. Then there was the money to remodel it, and they paid me very well, even though I didn't ask. They did not like for me to do it for free. One thing I was able to do from my heart was the best job I could. Everybody said I was doing a good remodeling job. Besides, I was out of my mind without sleep, everything was so nice. Of course, they needed many things for the house, and I was just happy to help.

The lady who lived in the house next door to the one my daughter and her husband was renting became a really good friend. She found me a job in the neighborhood, because she said, "I recommended you like I've known you forever because I've never seen anyone work that hard and do such an amazing, perfect job." So, she introduced me to her family. She had lived in Anchorage for thirty-five years, and she had friends all over. So, I was even able to stay in Alaska, and I got a job. And every day, I had more friends. I would go back and forth to Home Depot, for some reason; and I have friends at Home Depot as if I had been going there for the last ten years.

I had a chocolate lab. I already mentioned how I brought my chocolate lab when he was around ten or eleven weeks old, and how happy he was to see my son-in-law. I said, "I hope this is the boy." Thank God, I was right. Of course, I had a special dog. He was now nine years old. We went for walks every morning and evening in the neighborhood and everyone said hi to me like I had lived in this neighborhood for ten years. I wondered how everyone knew me. Everyone was so nice: nice neighborhood, nice people, friendly people. Even if I went to Home Depot or Lowe's and ordered or signed something, and said I was Frank, everyone called me by name, and I'd just say, "My God, believe it, I am at home!"

Everything went so well. My son-in-law started his dream job as a professor. He was so nice to me. He wanted to introduce his boss to me and show me where he worked. He had a beautiful office with a nice view and had a nice boss. My daughter still had to study for the last test to get her medical license. So, for about four or five months, she didn't work because she had to study for the test. So, I helped as much as I could.

As I said earlier, I used to go home and play with my kids when they were little. I used to feel younger and didn't feel tired. At that time, I wasn't old; I was just a twenty-five-year-old. But this time, I was a sixty-two-year-old. Believe it or not, when I played with my three grandkids, I was like a fourth kid. I wasn't tired. I didn't feel like a my age; I felt like a kid. I went under the table and all over the house and backyard. Then we went to the park. I was okay. I'm diabetic, but otherwise, I did pretty well. I didn't walk like a sixty-two-year-old man. I walked like another kid next to my grandkids. I was so happy and didn't feel tired. I'd watch Csoko, my lab. He'd walk, and I saw his extremely happy face. Everything was going fine.

Of course, my daughter was working hard and still studying. After many years, she was still studying. Of course, she took the test, and finally, she got licensed to practice medicine. You know, as I mentioned, getting a medical degree is not a piece of cake, and not fun. She would go to work, and then I would see her coming home with her computer and doing a lot of work at home. Plus, Mark had an evening class on Tuesday and Thursday. Mark's parents — his mother or father, mostly his mother — would come over. She and I would take care of everything. I would help as much as I could. So, everything went very well.

Then winter came. It was fun for the kids because they had never been in the snow. It had also been a long time since my daughter had been in the snow. But I grew up in a country that had a lot of snow in the winter. I had also stayed in New York for a couple years, so I wasn't afraid of shoveling snow. I liked to clear the front of the house, at least ten feet of the road in front of the house.

Everyone driving by slowed down and looked. "What's going on? The neighbor is shoveling the snow off the road."

One guy asked me, "Are you going to shovel the snow off the road, too?"

I said, "Well, I don't like to have to park my car in the snow, or my son-in-law's parents parking out front in the center of the road. So, of course, I shovel the snow all the way to the center of the road, and to the curb and the walkway."

The postal worker said, "Everybody needs to shovel at least the driveway."

But not everyone shoveled the snow in Alaska. I didn't know why, but that was okay. Here, it wasn't like we got a couple inches of snow, and then the sun came up and the snow was gone. Here, we got a couple feet of snow, and it stayed waiting for another couple feet of snow.

This year, we haven't gotten as much snow, but, last winter, we got about five or six feet of snow. I enjoyed it and was so happy to do the shoveling of the driveway and take care of the house inside and do what needed to be done.

I was always happy to do help this beautiful family because it didn't matter if they both had a Ph.D.; they would probably work harder. They had three beautiful kids. It wasn't always fun, especially for my daughter. She was a medical doctor. She needed to do a lot of computer work for her patients. My son-in-law was working, too, to set up what he would teach the next day. So, he has a lot of hard work to do, also.

When it came time, in the evening, to make dinner, I was amazed at how much my son-in-law helped his wife. In the morning, he woke up and made pancakes. Of course, my daughter needed more time to get dressed. She went to work at eight. She couldn't just jump out of bed and into the car. She had to dress professionally. She was a natural woman and beautiful, too. She dressed nice and simple. My son-in-law's mother had a Ph.D. and had an amazing personality. Mark's father was a retired teacher. It was amazing how approachable his father was.

Winter was going well. It was the first cold weather of the season. We had to wear gloves and learn day by day.

My niece was still waiting for me in New York. I left three years ago, and said I was going back the next spring. First, I stayed in Davis at my daughter's. I had a plan to move to Michigan. Then my daughter decided to move to Alaska, and I said, "Well, okay, I'll go to Alaska and paint your house, and in October, I'll go to New York."

Then I was unable to leave my family. I stayed all winter and said I would go in the spring. Then I got busy doing this and doing that. Then a neighbor lady I met named Bea wanted me to remodel her house. I redid everything: the basement, all new doors, new tile, and everything. It was a lot of work. Plus, I had a hard time leaving my three beautiful grandkids; my daughter and her husband and his family just kept me here. I didn't want to get heartbroken, as I knew I would be if I left the family. So, I stayed and was so happy to stay with this beautiful family.

So, I now end my daughter's chapter. I am now sixty-three. I turn sixty-four next year on May 18th, but I feel thirty-five or forty. I'm not tired. I play with my grandkids like I'm another child. In the morning — it doesn't matter if it's 2:00 or 5:00 in the morning — my grandkids are screaming that they are happy to see me. We play together like I am the fourth kid because I'm so happy to spend every minute with my grandkids and my daughter and her husband because this family is just beautiful.

Chapter 8

Son

I'd like to work on my son's chapter right now. He was born on February 24, 1975. His mother did not have any complications during pregnancy. Everything went so well and she delivered him without any complications. He was a beautiful newborn baby and thank God he was so healthy. Everything was in order as there was nothing unusual and no problems.

He was a beautiful child. I didn't know before he was born if he was a boy or a girl. But again, when my daughter was born, to me, it did not make a difference whether it was a boy or a girl. But that day ws a beautiful day for me. I had a daughter and a son.

He came home after four days because in my country you must stay in the hospital for four days. My daughter was so happy for her baby brother. I just couldn't tell you how happy I was about everything going well and having a new member in the family.

My kids' mother, for some reason, showed a difference of attention in her son in the beginning. But the reason I gave for this – and I won't judge it – she was not happier for a son or a daughter. But the reason I mentioned it was because that might happen in the beginning and I was going to tell you more of this story later.

Of course, my kids' mother stayed home. My kids had a peaceful life. They didn't need to wake up early to go to a daycare. She didn't need to go to work. She constantly had to raise two children and clean the house. But I helped her clean the house a lot.

I didn't have time to cook. I know how to cook because I learned. When I was a small child, I needed to learn how to cook. But with cooking, I didn't have time to do it because I was the only member working in the family. But sometimes I made the special food I learned from my mother. My kids' mother, when I married her, didn't know how to cook, so I taught her. Her cooking came out very well.

My son was born in February. And then in May, I went on a trip. I wouldn't say it was a vacation. I went to United States to visit a family member from my father's side. I had a dream even when I was nine. Again, some relatives were here when I came to the United States because on my father's side was very big and some of them came to Canada, Australia, and all over the world. My father had eighteen sisters and brothers, so it was a huge family.

When I visited the United States, I stayed over there two and a half months. I went back and my kids' mother did a beautiful job taking care of the kids. Of course, as I mentioned, she lived in a home I built which had one and a half bedrooms – a little cottage for a little building site. I changed a shop to a residency. Her mother did a beautiful job. She helped her a lot. My twin sister also helped her a lot while I stayed in the United States.

I returned to Hungary and I just worked day by day. I worked and everything went very well. But I saw it — my wife was closer to my son, and vice versa. But I wasn't disappointed. I gave him love for a child.

In our beginning, I went to a farm. My parents had a farm I didn't have yet. Later on, I had a chicken and a dairy farm. But already It had begun that, for some reason, my wife, did not want my son to work on a farm, and, in turn, he was happier to stay home. So, I accepted it. But she didn't tell my daughter not to work hard and stay home. But I didn't think so since she wanted to keep my daughter at home.

My daughter couldn't wait until Saturday and Sunday to come to the farm. On any school vacation she had, my daughter liked to spend as much time as she could to stay on the farm. I raised my children without buying a bunch of toys. They only had a few toys. I always found out a way to make things happen so the kids were not bored.

I went home all the time at noon. In my country, we had two hours for a major lunch in the day. But we ate in the morning and then also ate in the evening. But the biggest lunch was at noon. I went home at noon. I spent the time with my beautiful children. We had lunch together. I played with my children and I used that time to take a nap — a fifteen to twenty-minute nap. It just came out very well all of the time.

I had a working colleague and friend I had already met. His name was Steve. He had an auto repair shop but at the same time I already had my own business. I was always home around about 6:00 P.M. I mentioned earlier in my daughter's chapter at 6:00 to 6:30 there was a special children's show on TV. That time in my country we didn't have a twenty-four-hour TV channel. We only actually had one channel and it always started about 3:30 or 4:30 P.M. and then shut down about 11:00.

But there was a special kids' show about 6:00 to 6:30. After that we took a bath and I did my two beautiful children together. They mostly went to bed at eight and mostly used to it. Actually, I am a morning person, not an evening person. I used to have to go to bed about 9:30.

And mostly I raised kids, too, at five in the morning. It didn't matter how much I wanted to stay in the bed, I just couldn't make it because I was raised and I grew up never staying in bed later than five. I don't think I mentioned it in my daughter's chapter, but still it was mostly like a very peaceful morning. Not just to hurry after I wake up, but to always spend one hour in the home. I went to work.

As I mentioned earlier, after I started my own auto repair business, I also worked with Steve. I decided to start my own farm to raise geese and chicken. I always much I was working and what my life really was to wake up every morning. I had the dairy farm. I woke up not at 4:30, 5:00. I woke up 3:00 am and then went to bed at 9:30 or 10:00. I wasn't doing that for two weeks or one week. That was for 365 days. Every day I had to wake up at 3:00 A.M. to get everything in order.

Then, as I already mentioned in my daughter's chapter, a school teacher started to give my daughter a hard time. My son was just in first elementary but I already knew he had one teacher who was part of a whole family that were very strong communists. I knew she hated my family from father's side. Everybody was so rich and they did not like it at all since they were communists.

But I mean, I did not like it, but I was not fighting against communism. I just stayed away from them and those kinds of politics. But she made a difference for my son like another child. Because my son got this hard time within school and my daughter's teacher, of course mostly all the teachers were communist because even someone not a communist, they worked hard to get the job. But I'm not going to talk about the politics i my son's chapter very much. It was only to help me immigrate to the United States.

But mostly I had many possibilities to immigrate to other countries, but for some reason I chose United States. I didn't want to leave a family and immigrate myself and bring the whole family later to the United States. I work hard to get the whole family a passport and then immigrate to Austria. In Austria we applied to immigrate to the United States.

Again, I had a strong political reason to leave Hungary. Because my mother and youngest brother had a very difficult time on my farm. I do not want to talk about that on this chapter. I just wanted to mention it. But later I will tell you what it was.

When the time came in August 17, 1983, we left Hungary. I drove to the Austria border at midnight. We planned to drive to a border with the whole family at midnight, 11:00 to 12:00 A.M. Two people were waiting for me over there and helping the whole family going through a border. Because I was so close to my children, I found a way to be able to make it to leave myself and my children. It had to be to bring my kids' mother and myself, too.

After I went to a border, I told my son, and he was just a young child. But he knew because I told my daughter the same thing and my son. We left everything over there. I was so happy I took my dog, a longhaired dachshund dog.

My son hugged his mother and then he came and hugged me, too. He kissed me and said, "Thank you, Daddy. You did not leave me at home and you took me, too."

My whole family petted my kid's dog. His name was Dino. He hugged Dino, too. So, everything went very well.

I drove to Austria, and the next morning I found the immigrant office and then applied to immigrate to the United States. Everything went so well. Many people were waiting for at least a year to go anywhere in the world. But I had a very strong political reason to leave Hungary. I left very fast. On December 19th, the whole family made it to United States.

In the United States, as I mentioned in my daughter's chapter, I went to New York and my kids weren't = happy over there. Even my dog wasn't happy over there, especially because of the winter, as it was very windy. Some winters were mild while some winters were very strong. But that winter was an especially hard winter around Christmas in New York.

My kids' mother had a relative in California. They made phone calls back and forth. It was fine we would get visit in California. My wife, she called her and she was so anxious and so happy to know family members that immigrated to United States. In the next couple of days, she bought tickets for our family.

Even then, I started a job in an auto repair shop in New York. I got the job at an auto repair job like what car I knew very well. But again, and always I did what was best for my family. So, in January 15, 1984, I made it to the Oakland airport in California. A beautiful family was waiting for me and drove to Redding in Northern California.

I found out over there I was unable to make enough money to raise my children, paying for a new car and many other things. I came to feeling very much that I would make more money to go back to New York. I met a Hungarian lady a couple of days before Christmas and I had her number and everything.

I told my wife, "I'm sorry. California is so beautiful. Everything is green, but maybe I need to go back to New York to make a little money while you stay here." I called her and told her what had happened.

She said, "Wait, no, no, no. Don't come back to New York. I have a relative in Monterey, California." She said Monterey was the nicest place on Earth. She phoned back and forth.

In March, I went down to Monterey on the Greyhound bus. I met a Catholic priest there and he introduced me to another Hungarian family.

I had a house for my family. I got a car. Somebody gave me a Volkswagen van. I already talked about that. I made the house that had been empty for a couple of years to be a nice place for my family. After about a month and a half, I went back to pick up my family.

Of course, every weekend I drove to northern California to spend the time with our children. That was about 640 miles back and forth. One way was about 320 miles. Actually, quite close to 640 or 650 miles. But I had to do that to spend time with my family on a weekend.

So, everything went very well and my son and my daughter were just so happy to play with my wife. I finished the house. I already had a Volkswagen van. So, on the weekend the family and my dog would fit in the van. I would travel up to Reading, pick up the whole family, and bring them down to a beautiful small house. It was a small house, but I made it so very nice because I already knew construction in my country, Hungary. I made it. It was just beautiful and had a lot of color.

I brought my family. I met many Hungarian people. There were about 500 Hungarians in Monterey County. But from the people I met, everybody was just so happy to finally meet my family when I brought them Monterey. All the people gave us pots and pans and sheets and beds. Everything really went so well.

The same thing when I got a Volkswagen and had the Volkswagen van and there was a problem with the engine, but I fixed it. I also had an automobile that was an Oldsmobile 88 that was built in 1968. An old lady owned it, but she got sick and she couldn't drive it anymore, so I got that car.

I did very well for a construction and auto mechanics. Everything went so well. I painted houses and replaced roofs and at the same time I worked on I rebuilt engines for Star Motor Mercedes. Everything just went so peacefully well.

In the United States, more and more I saw and felt a difference my wife had between our daughter and son. But again, I accepted it. I was working hard so my daughter was not able to find out about that. But, to me, my daughter was so nice and helpful to me, I didn't feel differently. I gave more love to my daughter because she's much closer to me and I worked hard to give more love to my son to realize there was no difference.

He did very well at school. He was a very good student, but he needed to work much harder to get good grades in a school, unlike my daughter. Studying was easy for her. But then again, that didn't happen for everybody. For some, it didn't matter how they hard work, they didn't have good grades in school and weren't able to get it. For others, all they have to do was look at the paper, study, and then get a good grade. But this was nothing unusual.

Both my kids worked at Fisherman's Grotto on Fisherman's Wharf at a restaurant. A guy liked to sell the roses for people. And so, my kids stayed over there and made a couple of bucks by selling roses to people. This family was actually from Pakistan, but their nationality didn't matter. Everybody was so nice to my family and to me, too. My son got to the point where he was selling the flowers, but I helped him every morning to deliver the newspaper called the *Monterey Herald*. There was one Hungarian friend who worked on the Monterey Herald. I wanted to teach my children how they needed to do something to earn money. Not because I accepted or I needed that money but that my children had earned. At a young age, I tried to teach him to do something so he would know how he needed to work for money.

I never kept the money or wanted it. Always my son and my daughter wanted to keep it and put in a little box to save the money. I never, ever needed to use that money to buy something or toys or anything. Just for them save it for the future.

My daughter worked in a couple nursing homes. She was interested in working in them. Actually, in her chapter I forgot to mention about that nursing home. But my son did different interesting jobs. He worked at an animal shelter where they took dogs and cats and that type of thing. He had a small dream to becoming veterinarian – taking care of animals. But his grades and everything were, at first, always low to start at that school. But his grades were not that high to able to make it because he was unable to study the same things as his sister. He helped a vet, but he was not earning money. Whereas my daughter helped at a nursing home to make old people happy and she liked to go to the hospital also. But that was voluntary.

My son worked at the Mi Casa store. He started making money. My daughter also worked one place at a nursing home — a part-time job that was couple hours a week. I think she did about six hours a week. At that time, she made a little money. But, she did voluntary work at a nursing home because everybody didn't want to miss her and love her.

Actually, in her chapter, I did not mention this, but my son finished eighth grade. He got a pretty good chunk of money from many places – the Knights of Columbus and Bank of America and everything. He had very high grades and almost straight A's. But he got a bonus check from many other places. But my daughter got more than $10,000 from Bank of America and Knights of Columbus and many other places. My daughter got one month's free vacation to East Germany. She finished high school, I mentioned in her chapter.

My son worked at Mi Casa. At same time he chose to go to a firefighter school. His mother said he was a handsome boy and a lot of firefighters were handsome. Firefighting is a very dangerous, hard job. But sometimes it's a very peaceful life and he did not need to make his hands dirty. I didn't know that. My wife said that. She encouraged him to be a firefighter, but he also loved going to firefighter school, too. I said yes and just accepted it again. I said, "Well, you want it that way so go ahead. Do it that way."

So let's go back to when he was working in Mi Casa store and he met his first girlfriend. Her name was Danielle and she was a beautiful girl. My son met his first girlfriend. But, I hoped she would be my son's future wife because my son hadn't had a girlfriend before. Also, he was a very shy boy because he mostly stayed with his mommy. But it didn't matter. He was a beautiful son.

He didn't know how to date, but this girl was so sharp and so sweet. She knew how to handle it to change my son's life and give up loving and hugging his mommy all the time; he needed somebody else in order to start his own life and to know how to make or give love to a woman.

They did pretty good. But here's start sad part. She was a little bit over-weight and not his mother's favorite person. She worked very hard to stop my son from dating this girl. Then my son started to feel disappointed and thought about what he was going to do. I talked to Danielle. I had a feeling my son was not just going to movies. My son was not dating before, but I saw he was a little different and had love for this lady. He gave more attention to Danielle.

His mother worked harder to stop him from becoming closer to Danielle. I didn't know if it was because she felt like she was losing her son. I didn't know. I didn't want to go into the details.

Danielle went to school to become a teacher and finished her degree. My son finished firefighter school but received some bad news about a firefighter who was burned in a forest fire. People died in Monterey County. One friend's son was burned in a fire in New York. He just finished firefighter school and got the job in Chester County. But he never worked like a firefighter. Before he started the work, he quit. He worked full-time in Mi Casa store.

His girlfriend went to school in Santa Rosa. It was a very big step for my son. He worked for Rohnert Park in a Mi Casa store. My son and his girlfriend rented an apartment in Rohnert Park, California that was close to Santa Rosa. He worked full-time and she went to school and helped him to pay bills. I bought a car for my son and I helped where I could to fix the car.

I did not mention this earlier. My son had a yellow lab. Because he moved in an apartment that did not allow pets, I took care of his dog, and her name was Sandy. Everything went so well.

They had lived together without getting married, and I was not happy to see that. But they were not the only children living together. So, I agreed. But, of course, my wife was extremely hardworking, too, and unhappy to see them living together. It was not because they were not married, but because she didn't like her.

I always told my son, "I know how much you love your mother and how close you are, but if you want to do more than date your girlfriend, and you think you'll be able to continue your life with her in marriage, don't listen to your mom. Mommy will try to find the best way to accept it. But do what is best for you." And he did.

My son's girlfriend, Danielle, actually went to school in Santa Rosa to become a teacher and lived in Rohnert Park. She had two more years of school and continued in Chico State University, California. They lived in Paradise. Of course, I helped him to move. When they were in Paradise they rented a duplex. They let him bring his dog over there. So, he had his dog with him now. I took the dog for about two years. He got his dog back and lived in a very nice place.

They were not married at this time, but still living together. She was just so nice to me and everything went so well.

Finally, Danielle finished school at Chico State University. She got a job and moved to Manteca, California. Anyway, it was during this time while they were in the middle of moving to the new place, they had a wedding and got married.

I'm going to put in a very sad story. I bought a new suit and was so happy to see that. I couldn't say how much I waited for them to get married. Of course, his mother fought against that day not to happen. But I did not say anything negative. I just stayed away from my son and his mother's situation.

I just told my son, "Do it, but do what is best for you. You love this girl and you feel you're able to continue your life with her. Don't listen to your mom. It does not mean you're a bad boy or doing anything wrong."

Now I never liked parents telling a child which person – girl or boy, it didn't matter – would be better to marry.

And then, I dress up and accepted it and was so happy to go to a wedding. I had a P.O. Box, but don't ask me why. Friday afternoon I went. Sometimes in the whole week, I did not check it. Mostly I went to a P.O. Box on Saturday or Sunday to the middle of the week. I would just go over there Saturday or Sunday to pick up the mail. Some mail came to my house but my own business had a P.O. Box. Later I will tell you probably why it had to be to a P.O. Box.

For some reason somebody wanted me to pick up the mail on Friday afternoon. It was very sad. When I picked up the mail, I saw the mail was coming to my name. And then on the top left corner, I read my son's name; Csaba with the middle name of Ferenc. It was Csaba Ferenc Baba, his letter. I said, so my son and my future daughter-in-law already gave me a card to come to the wedding.

I already worked. His mother was not working. I never had lots of money because I helped the whole family and my daughter. I helped him with a car and as much I could. I was not really able to put a lot of money in savings, but everything was difficult everywhere.

I needed to open it. I opened this letter. You guys are not going to believe it. My son said, "I don't want you to come to my wedding."

It was very hard for me. I wasn't going to cry, but he damaged my heart. So, I accepted it. I had a lot of friends and mostly worked on Saturdays all the time, too, in my auto repair shop because I had an auto repair shop. I told everybody, well, I was not in a shop because I had a very interesting day on my son's wedding.

I lived in Monterey. I went in the car to the beach and just sat there. Then I prayed and asked for God to help me heal on this very sad day. But I accepted it and did not get mad or change anything towards my son. I said, well, I need to accept it.

And so, they continued life in Manteca and didn't really ask me to visit him. It was okay. Someday it was coming and my son's wife worked as a teacher in Manteca; she's a beautiful girl and a very nice person. She paid a bill and my son went to school to study psychology and did very well. I knew they had a beautiful marriage. Not because I had been to visit, because they had not really asked me. That did not mean she was not asking me to visit in Manteca.

But a year later, I found where they live exactly in Manteca. I said, well, like or not, I was going to visit to him. I used God in my chapter in my book. But I felt God made it happen for a reason – a car and then a house and dog and everything – and forced or changed my son's mind. Not my daughter-in-law's, since she was always so nice to me, super nice to me, and she gave me love and hugs. My son was so happy to call me to help him.

I told my son, "I don't know whether or not you don't have any idea how much I miss you. Every day I'm working on it. I go to sleep dreaming about visiting you. I open my eyes in the morning and think it's another day. How can I tell my son and daughter-in-law, 'Here I am. I am happy to see you.'?"

My son called me on Friday morning, saying, "We have a problem. I need help. You don't mind coming to my place?" They had rented a place that was a small house in Manteca. Actually, it was a duplex, too; like an apartment complex, not a condominium, but a duplex that had two apartments together.

I went over and was so happy to see them. It was a nice place and I was finally able to give them hugs. I got my son back. After a year of marriage, I got to congratulate them for the wedding. Everything went so well. My daughter-in-law was a wonderful teacher.

My son finished psychology school where he got a bachelor's degree. At that time, he got a master's degree. He started working in Stockton, California. He found out it was better he got a bachelor's degree for psychology. They were good at saving money and bought a house in Stockton, California. It wasn't too far from Manteca.

My son worked as a psychologist. My daughter-in-law made pretty good money as a teacher because she did a special program in school to get more money to teach where the kids have problems. I'm not going on about these details, but she did make pretty good money. My son was already making money with psychology, and at the same chose to go to school in addition to working.

After a couple of years, he got a bachelor's degree for psychology. They had a beautiful marriage. A lot of people, of course, had nice marriages, beautiful marriages. But they were peaceful with no complications and a great time together. I saw both of them were so happy.

She had a problem with being overweight, but she was a beautiful girl. Not just because she was my son's wife, but definitely she's a beautiful lady; he's a very handsome and nice boy. Everything went very well.

They started to think about having a child. The first pregnancy did not go well, and she lost her baby. After about a year, she tried again and got pregnant a second time. She had another problem; she was unable to make it to nine months. The baby was born at six and a half months, and I think she was only one and a half pound. But she had all kinds of complications. The hospital did a beautiful job and saved her.

After about three months, they were able to bring her home, a newborn baby, a daughter, and her name was Kaycee.

My son worked very hard. He was always a hard worker and so happy, and finally had a child. Before bringing her home, my son's wife was in a car accident. She had a serious problem with her foot and right arm. But thanks to God, she survived.

But the reason I mentioned it was because my son saw how hard I worked and how much I did to make our family happy. He knew he needed to handle the situation and help her heal from her injuries – surgery for her foot, leg, and arm. The baby was finally home and he had a peaceful life.

Now I am finished, so this is my son's chapter. His last chapter with my daughter but that was only because he and his mother and wanted it that way.

And I accepted it. I was amazed at how well my son had done in life; he had a child and a house and a peaceful life. He was a really hardworking person, from what I had seen. Even his wife was an amazingly hard worker and a nice wife. My son never drank alcohol or smoked. His wife didn't drink alcohol and didn't have any bad habits. She had a normal life like it was supposed to be.

Chapter 9

Dog

I would like to make a chapter for my dog. So far, I have not talked about my special dog.

In my life, I always had a dog and even mentioned it in the book earlier my first nice dog was born on September 9, 1956. I enjoyed it and we lived together for seventeen years. I already mentioned he died in my arms. Even in his last minute, he sat in my lap, licked my face, and then in another second, he died.

I had a dog I brought from Hungary. I helped out my son. The dog I brought from Hungary was a long-haired dachshund. He died when he was fourteen years old. My son got a yellow Lab and enjoyed it when he was home. He moved in with his girlfriend before they married, so he did not have a chance to bring his dog to his apartment in Rohnert Park, California. So, I took care of her for two or three years. It was a minimum of two years, but I think he had a chance to take it the third year because they moved to Chico and then they had a house. They rented a house and were able to bring the dog around 2002.

I'm going back to my other special dog. In 2000, I had in my mind to get a chocolate Lab or some kind of brown dog. I will tell you a bit before I step into my dog story. I will tell you how many years earlier I decided to have a dog, a brown dog.

Back in Hungary, I had one, real story. In Hungary, there was a law. It's similar to having a county. For example, this area was like Siskiyou County or

Monterey County. The mayor was going hunting from one property to another property. It's not allowed. It was only possible to hunt in your own county. No city; I'm talking about a county like Shasta County. So, what happened was this man went hunting and he had a brown dog. He was the mayor and another mayor and his dog ran to his county border and shot and killed his dog. But for this man and this mayor that dog was very special for him. The mayor killed his dog. So, he saw he killed his dog and he said, "Dog life, change to dog," and he shot and killed the mayor. It's just a bit I step in this story and then he had a brown dog.

I saw this movie because I was a twenty-two-year old. The movie's name was *Black City* because he killed the mayor and then everything in the county and the city was dark for three days – no light or anything. It came out as really big history and a big deal. But, of course, this mayor got the death penalty. I saw his dog. I only wanted to talk about this a little bit. I'm not going into details. I saw really how this dog was his favorite. I always said someday I would have a brown dog also.

I used it many times. It did not mean I was using God to step into another story or an excuse for God. I used it because I was raised Catholic, so I used the word – it's God. I always said, "God, give me this brown dog." What happened was, at that time, I was in Shasta County in California. I picked up a *Thrifty Nickel* newspaper on Thursday and found one Labrador dog in the newspaper. It was a female.

I went over there. He was gone on the weekend and everything and for some reason I made it on Monday afternoon to buy this dog. It was a cute dog and she already loved me and sat in my lap and everything. And then I got there. I found out I forgot my wallet in my studio apartment above my shop. I said, "I like this dog, but I left my wallet at home." I lived at the shop at this time.

I went back to the shop and somebody came over. He had an emergency with his car because he wanted to go on a long trip. Something was wrong with his car and he wanted me to check it. So, I checked his car and more; it cost me almost two hours at this time to check his car. I went back with the money to buy that cute brown female Labrador.

He said, "Sorry." He waited for half an hour, but somebody asked him and he took the dog.

I said, "Okay. God wanted it that way."

The next Thursday came out another Thrifty Nickel and then I saw over there somebody had a dog for sale, a Labrador puppy. Of course, I wanted to buy a puppy. I called the person immediately on Thursday. I picked up the newspaper about 11:00 A.M. I called, but nobody answered the phone. I left a message.

The person came back around about 4 or 5 o'clock and told me he had a dark brown Canadian Lab. Before he had lived in Boise, Idaho he and his family moved to Redding, California in north California at that time. I had two shops, so I was over in Redding and then I thought I, definitely I need one puppy. Female or male, it didn't matter, just a dark brown chocolate lab.

I knew this Canadian Lab. It had a big head. They already told me the father was 137 pounds, and the mother was around 100 pounds. It was a huge and a very nice dog. Of course, I wanted to buy a female on Monday. That one was just $150 and I paid him $700. But thank God it didn't matter if it's $150 or $700. But really, I did not care about a paper.

He said everything was fine and then this family was at Lake Tahoe for some reason. I am not going into details. I was not sure exactly why they were in Lake Tahoe. They just moved to Redding, California. They said they'd be back sometime Saturday or Sunday. She called me on Friday around 1:00 P.M. She said if I was serious about buying a dog, it's okay if I went over there to look at the dog this afternoon because a lot of people were calling and for some reason they were going back one day earlier even. But this meant they would make it back in Redding on Friday afternoon.

I said, "Okay, of course, definitely." Because it seemed to her I was definitely interested in a dog. I said, "I definitely want one. I am ready to buy it." This was on December 23, 2004.

I went over there and he had six puppies, but only five had papers. He said that one had no papers and was just $300 and it was not dark brown. He had one that was a female, and also a male — big head and dark brown.

He said, "Sorry, but that one just sold hours ago."

I said, "Well, okay."

He said he had one puppy that when he has born that just all the time after he start to walk, he came out to take a pee and then he would go back to sleep. Almost all the time it was sleeping. So, he picked up a dog cage and, yes, he was there and he was dark brown, big head and everything. It was a beautiful puppy.

I said, "Okay, I want him."

She said, "Okay, just a minute. I will go to talk to my husband," because I talked to both the wife and husband, but the family was busy over there because they had just moved.

I was talking to the wife before she went inside and her husband came out; I had to think about how I was going to do it. At that time, I had money, so there was no problem. I picked up this puppy and put him on my shoulder and when I picked him up; he opened his eyes and was yawning. He turned to sleep and snored.

I told him, "Look at it. He has gone to sleep. Is it okay if I hold him while I go to my car to pick up my wallet to pay for him?"

He said, "Of course."

So, I went to the car, brought in my wallet, and I paid for him. At that time, he was seven weeks old.

The guy said, "Are you coming back to pick him up in two or three weeks?"

I said, "No, I don't think so, because look at this dog. He's sleeping. He is next to my neck and snoring. I don't think he wants to go back to a cage."

He said, "No problem. He's already eating and drinking milk, so he's okay."

I said, "Of course I know I need to make him okay. Even if he does not drink milk, I'm going to teach him."

This was a nice family who took care of the dog, but not in the way I take care of dogs and animals. But I didn't judge them and this was his business, so I gave him $700. He did not come down on the price. I asked him, "Is it $600?"

He said, "No." He said he had had many phone calls while selling this dog immediately after I saw the parents. They were a beautiful mother and father. And then I bought it. So, I went home.

He is dreaming now and looks like he knows I'm talking about him; he is here next to me. He still sleeps about 95% of the time. He's nine and still sleeps all the time.

I took him home. You probably could guess that when you buy a dog or a puppy and bring it home, then it cries and has a hard time.

He never ever cried or looked for his mommy. But I was already on the way home and stopped to see a vet. I bought a special formula just in case for puppy milk. For everything else, I went to a store. I bought milk recommended for a baby. Everything was in order for him to continue his life.

I didn't want to teach him to sleep with me in a bed. So, in the first week, I slept on the floor with him and always put him on my heart. When I was driving a car, he always slept and stayed in my lap. But, it was so interesting, when I left him in the car from the shop or home, he came sitting in my lap. He went to sleep in one minute. He would not even raise his head until I stopped the car and when I got to my destination.

That one was on December 23rd and he was seven weeks old before Christmas. I just enjoyed it. It was really an amazing Labrador puppy. I had a hard time because the first time I picked it up, he was so sleepy because he had firm hair on it because it was a little bit fat. Not too fat for a puppy, but it was a very interesting, cute puppy. Everybody was screaming when they saw him over how beautiful he was. So that was on December 23rd.

Of course, I love cats, too. So, I had a mother cat and she delivered three kitty cats. They were barely opening their eyes and something happened. The mother went someplace and did not come home; a car probably hit her or something; I'm not sure exactly what had happened to her.

I thought, all right, I have a puppy — a two-month-old puppy — and now I had three cats that have barely opened their eyes and no mother. One was black, one was a tabby, and one was grey. But that one was not just a wild cat. I thought somebody over there called it a "barn cat" or I forget the exact name. But one lady said the cat came from the wild. It was very strong and got sick very few times. But once it loves an owner or had person to own it, it's very friendly to them.

It was very protective of its owner and then it almost acts like a dog when somebody came to my house. The mother was similar that I saw that with her.

But it mostly was someplace hiding in the shop when anybody came over. Nobody needed protecting.

The mother was gone. I went to a vet again and knew her very well, because I worked on her Mercedes; she's my veterinarian and was going to take care of Csoko. I went over and explained to them what has happened.

She said, "I know you and your heart. I know you're going to save these three cats."

It was a lot of work, but she explained everything to me. She gave me a special formula needed for these kitty cats. I bought the formula, along with a bottle to feed them. You know, it's for a cat like feeding with very small rubber. I think you call it bottle. A little bottle for feeding an infant child but also a dog or a cat and it's possible using a very small one. I have a couple of them.

It was hard to believe it but these cats, about a couple of days, they realized they had no more mother, but chose me that I am this mother. I fed them and helped to take a pee and everything. I had to buy some plastic and put that on my shirt and then I lay down and on my chest were the three cats. I fed them at same the time. The time had come to feed the cats and they would climb up on my pants and asked me for food.

So, I named him Csoko. I got my brown lab puppy. This was the reason my email and almost everything – password, everything – I used his name a different way, one way or another way. The extra number was changing.

I had these three cats. All three are male and then I would not actually call it a black kitty and a tabby and a grey. I called it grey, but I gave them a Hungarian name. But mostly, I just called them in my language – Kitty Mitty. All three when they were running away, I would say this Kitty Mitty and all three of them would just run over. Almost all three had the same name. Listen to all three the same name all the time and all three of them running in at the same time. I had to pet them. I had these cats because I raised them amazingly, extremely well. I had had so much fun in my shop with my three cats and a Csoki. I called him Csokikam. His nickname was Csoko. Sometimes I said "Csoki Moka" and my one grandson called him "Csoki Moka".

I was still at that time separated from my ex-wife. At that time in 2002, I filed a separation and then I finalized the divorce in 2006. So, it's very interesting. One day she came over to the shop with a man. I had already seen them. I had bad memories about the whole thing. I am sorry. It's very sad. And, believe it or not, I saw my three cats and my Csoko didn't want her.

It was about a couple months before we finalized it, actually. It was in October, 2005 that she came over. I got Csoko in 2004 and then all three cats and Csoko didn't want them to come in my shop or my house. Because above my shop I had a studio I made over there to live in.

It was very interesting. I always had these three beautiful cats and nobody was able to pet these cats. I mean, only one man had come over there and got closer. This guy had a Mercedes and his sister came over there.

She said, "Are you sure you need all three cats?"

I said, "Of course I need these three cats."

They started getting closer to this cat, especially the man. But the black, tabby, and grey cat did not let him touch it. But the man was crazier for the grey cat. It's a huge grey cat and beautiful and he said his sister was always dreaming for a nice grey cat.

One day the cat was missing. I bet you he took the cat because they wanted it badly. But still I was sad. But that way it was about after three years I had it and then it left. I have just only a black and a tabby cat. It was a long cat story, I will stop talking about that for now, but I will continue it in just a bit. I will mention it what has happened on how I stepped into having a cat.

I went everyplace. It's very funny how I already mentioned that Csoki liked to sit in my lap and go places. He's more of a puppy, but of course he's a Labrador. It's a huge dog. He grew up and he never understood how come it was not able to sit in my lap anymore while I'm driving a car because I cannot use the steering wheel. I know especially California you cannot drive a car with a dog in the driver's seat. I knew that butt did it for him. Not just that, but right now it's even not allowed for a dog to sit on the passenger seat. It has to be sitting in a back seat.

Okay, so I'm talking about the back seat now because one time I drove to New York to see my niece to help her out with her house. She was divorced. She needed help. So, I was on the way to New York and I had two cats in the car, and Csoko, plus a lot of stuff. Csoko was a huge, 100-pound dog and liked to lie on the back seat and door to door.

I had a station wagon and put a lot of stuff in the back, but I didn't have enough room. I did put something on the back seat on one passenger side. I drove about eighty, maybe close to 100 miles and he's not able to lie down. He sat up. Anything he wanted he would always pet my arm to ask me to stop for water or food. He'd pet my arm and I'd stop. I gave him water. At the rest area, I stopped and walked with him and then went back to the car.

I drove ten or fifteen miles and he did it to me again. I told him, "Just don't tell me you're not happy because this baggage is next to you."

So next, I drove to a gas station and truck stop. I stopped there and had to reorganize the car because I knew one place which had small room in the back and it had over there a cat littering box and everything.

As I said, I had a station wagon and it had a rack. I put out stuff from the backseat and my daughter in the front seat and made it to put it on top of the car. He asked me something he wanted me to do for him, and finally he got it. He always a big way of saying: "Oh, thank you, finally you got it. Thank you very much. You know you got it what I was talking about." And then everything went well after I made a whole seat for him.

I drove so many different places. I went to New York, and then I had a house in Michigan. I also drove to Pennsylvania, but always with my two cats and Csoko.

One time somebody came over in my shop and I'm not going into this story. But he came over there. I will go a little bit back. Csoko, he had never, ever barked and he's never interested to play with another dog. He was always about four or five feet away. Even at the shop I went to one car to another car. He followed me like he's on a leash many times and laid down on the floor and sleep next to me.

But my two cats did it also. I worked on a car. First when I had three of them, I put down a little blanket or something and the three cats were sleeping next to a car with Csoko or Csoko on one blanket and the three cats on another blanket. Later two cats would follow me everywhere all the time, even at the shop or even now. But even when I went to take a shower in the bathroom, my three cats and Csoko came in the bathroom and lay down on the floor waiting for me to finish my shower. It's really very interesting.

This guy came over to the shop and it's the same thing. It's a bad memory I am not talking about at this time for this person. But again, this cat and dog knew it was not the right person to come over. He was barking. Even the three cats — at that time I had all three cats there — stood up next to Csoko and made like they were ready to do something to him. It's not going to leave in a minute.

I said, "I'd like to talk or listen to you, but look at it. I don't know how I can stop these three cats and Csoko and I don't think I am able to keep this dog and cats from attacking you. You better leave because I don't know what has happened. I am not going to touch you, but I'm not sure I'm able to stop Csoko or these three cats from doing something to you if you do not leave."

The man just turned around and left. But I just don't want to talk about it very much.

I will go into details for everything later, but I got diabetes around 2006. But I do not want to talk about it in my dog chapter.

I had diabetes, and the first time I got diabetic something happened. It was around 4:00 in the morning and I passed out. I remember it was about 6:30 or 6:45 when I woke up. Csoko was licking my face. Because nobody was over at the shop, I thought about what had happened and I was very weak and sick. But I said to myself I'm not too far from a hospital or I hope I make it to a hospital. And so, I sat sit in a car with Csoko. Of course, I left the three cats at home. I drove to the hospital. I saw where the building was, but barely; I lost sight of it. I just thought, Okay, twenty-five feet more. And then I remembered I was very close to the door. What I remember was about ten feet and then I passed out again. I found out my blood sugar was extremely high.

I am going to dive back into history because that started when it was at the first time when he would always take care of me. I called him my guardian angel. He was always next to me and so nice to me and gave attention to be sure everything was fine. Even when I was working under a car, he came over and watched the jack stand. He watched when I lifted up a transmission to starting a car. Even the cats came over and looked at it to make sure — because I worked by myself over there — that everything was going fine. Hard to believe, but I am telling you a true story.

I said I was going to the hospital. Nobody believed it. I drove over there after he made me feel better. It was amazing that the hospital let my dog Csoko stay in my room. That hospital was extremely nice. This time the hospital was called Redding Medical Center.

It was sad when I got diabetes. But always in my life I had been a hard worker, and then I found out in four or five years how I needed to handle my diabetes without medicine. I did a lot of exercises and, as I mentioned earlier, I did walk before even every morning for two miles and in the evening for two miles with Csoko. And then after I got diabetes, I walked more.

Csoko and I went to a park to play with the football. He's a master at playing football. He kicked with his nose many times, four or five times or more. He kicked a ball in the air. He had a special ball. He kicked the ball with his front foot. It's just amazing how much power and health and such a happy, nice day when this dog was given to me. Many times, I told my daughter, "If you are thankful for something I've done for you, don't thanks your father. Thanks, Csoko, because he's careful to make sure everything is going well with me."

At another time for some reason my blood sugar changed. After about five and a half years, I started using medicine in pill form. I did not have enough experience on how to use it. Plus, for me it's difficult for diabetes because if I took the pill and then I checked my blood sugar and I said, "This is the pill I need." But I did hard work and burned it faster, and then my blood sugar went low.

One time I passed out with the low blood sugar. And same thing, I knew when I opened my eyes I did not feel good and then I passed out. I opened my eyes. I said, "Okay, what is that? What is that?" He licked my face and then I just found out I was on the floor. So, he woke me up and then last time I did not need to go to the hospital. I realized what has happened. Immediately, I checked my blood sugar because it wasn't the first time that it had happened.

The second time I took it so I had a lot of side effects for pee and so I had a recommendation.

My sister in Hungary had diabetes, too. She said, "Why not just switch to insulin? It's not fun. It's a daily shot, but it has less side effects."

So, I did and of course it's another big step to learn how I need to use it. And if I was using more, not because of hard work and burn the sugar in my system faster because I am Type II, I was still not making some insulin in my system.

I had a problem. So, again, I passed out. At that time, it was in the evening and I probably passed out or something. My dog Csoko knew there was something wrong with daddy. So, what he did was he licked my face. I said, "Oh my, what has happened?" because otherwise he did not lick my face. I tried to wake up and then I found out I did and already knew my blood sugar was too low.

Another time I was working on a car in my shop and I did not feel good. Around Thursday, I went to a hospital. First year I saw the doctor, not the hospital. I said, "I do not feel good."

She said, "Well, it looks like you caught a cold because everybody has the flu or a cold at this time."

I said, "Okay."

She said, "You don't need medicine. Just go home and drink tea." And then she said, "Especially lemon tea will help you a lot."

So, I stopped in a store. I bought more lemon because I had one in my house but I said, "I'm going to drink lemon tea for twenty-four hours," and I put in double or three or four lemons in my tea because I felt terrible. By Friday evening, it was bad, on Saturday I was sick, and then Saturday evening I had to go to the emergency room and see a doctor. I got to go outside. The air or whatever made me maybe feel a little bit better. I explained to him what the last doctor said that it was a cold and this time he gave me cold medicine.

He said, "Go to Walgreens and buy one kind of cough medicine and take one tablespoon every four hours."

I went home and continued to feel sick, sick. On Monday morning around 10:00, I saw very interesting things and felt terrible and the room was spinning with me. I even had a very hard time to take a morning walk with Csoko. I said it would be better if I go out and then walk because I had a feeling I never had before. I had seen a bad thing and everything.

I did go out. I remember I went out of a room and then I walked about a half a mile and that one happened because I was not in my house. It happened in my shop because my shop had a studio. I came down and that area over there was mostly a commercial area. That's all I remember at this time, and then I woke up in a hospital and everybody was over there feeling sad.

Csoko was running around and he went in one cabinet shop and he was barking. And the people said, "Where did this dog come from?"

They said, "I don't know. I think I saw one guy waling with him before here, but I didn't pay attention if it was his dog or not or what has happened or why he has just come here." But he was barking. Normally, Csoko almost never barked.

One guy said, "I think he is pointing with his head and wants us to follow him." So, these two guys were following him. They walked about a half a mile, and he said, "Oh my God. This man is on the ground," and he immediately called an ambulance.

So, they took me to a hospital and of course I opened my eyes and I saw him at a hospital.

I liked Walmart, but I bought this carburetor cleaner at Walmart and did not read it. For some reason, I was always very careful, but I missed that sign on the can that you cannot use it inside a building. So, I used it inside. I am probably going in this story why I used it inside this building but I don't want to put it in my sweet dog's story what happened and why I got the blood poison from that carburetor cleaner.

Then came Tuesday, Wednesday, I felt a little bit better. On Thursday morning about 4:00 I started a cold fever because my blood pressure was extremely high and I had almost less than 50% chance to survive. But it was Thursday morning about 4 o'clock I had a cold feeling and shook and then I pushed the bell for a nurse. At first, she was not coming, and I knew I had more energy to say, "Help, help, help." At that time, I said that.

A nurse came and she pushed another button. I saw in the door three or four people run in and one guy was asking another one, "You know how you need to do that." This is what I remember and then I woke up. I went into a deep coma. Even my daughter finished public health and she had a convention in Maryland and she had a cell phone and they called her to come to the hospital because they were not sure her father was going to survive.

But, of course, I have to tell you they let Csoko stay. Even intensive care had a special room. He had one pillow and was not in a bed. He liked to sleep on a floor and on a pillow. But he didn't care. He wanted to stay in the same room where I was. It's a very kind hospital to let him to come in.

All the way up to today, I don't know what happened. If something happened to him, I don't know what had happened to him. I was not able leave the room or I went to a bathroom or I was going to another room in a house, all the way to today, he followed me everywhere. It's nice, but not very good because if something happens to me, he had a big problem, but just that.

That happened on a Thursday morning, and then I came back to life on Saturday and then I opened my eyes. I remember when I saw my daughter for the first time. Of course, I saw the dog in the same room and I realized I was in the same room from before. I saw my daughter and then I knew in a second. She already told me because she saw me and I wanted to raise my head to look under on the floor if Csoko was there or not.

But my daughter said, "Don't move. Just stay; he is here. I know you're looking for Csoko." And then she said, "But no, don't worry. He's here."

God gave me the power and let me continue my life because I had a feeling I still needed to help my daughter and my kids a lot and I had helped many other people. Csoko needed to be taken care of, too, because I was very important to him. Thank God I came back in a normal life. For a couple of months, this poison caused major damage to my system. But I had had a very healthy life. I never drank alcohol or smoked and I worked very hard to come back normal. Of course, I was also diabetic, but it's just sometimes somebody had something, it meant they learned to get used to it.

Everything went day by day and I had to finish working on cars. I got the point to give up working and staying in northern California. Somebody was always interested in buying my shop and business. One person helped me before and I told him I was not very happy to stay in Redding, California anymore. My niece lived in New York. I said, "Well, I would like to go to visit her."

This guy was interested in my business and shop. The first thing he did was to buy the business, but I helped him to get the property, too. But later, I will tell you it's a lot of things that happened before I decided at that point to step out of the auto repair business. But I do not want to talk about that one. Right now, I am talking about my dog's story.

On the way to New York, for some reason, I did not use 80. I used the Highway 24. I went to Indiana and many other nicer places. I had always driven the car and I had plenty of time to make it to New York. I was never in a hurry, but I wanted to see and always drove on Highway 40, Highway 20, 90, 80, Highway 50. I always liked to learn more about this beautiful country, the United States. I would always stop and meet a nice friend, and another nice friend.

I started not feeling well about noon. And then I got to the evening and I still did not feel well and got more and more sick. And then I was busy. I didn't know exactly where I was, so I just knew it was someplace in Indiana. I was driving and then way, way far away I saw it looked like there was one city over there.

I said, "Well, I hope I make it over there because it's come to the point where I do not feel good."

Five minutes later, I felt worse. Something happened to me and I lost a lot of blood and became anemic. I finally made it to a city. What was very interesting was my dog — believe it or not — came over and put his head on my neck. He licked my face. He was kicking my legs with his foot and my shoulder and then my arm and he was trying to keep me alive.

But I made it to the city and then I stopped the car and was looking around. I saw on a high post a sign for the hospital. I said, "I can't believe it." I said, "Okay, I hope I make it over there to that hospital." I started to drive the car over there and then at that time I was not even looking for a parking spot. I just drove closest to a door as much as I can. I saw it had a sign that said urgent care.

I drove over there and walked in the hospital. There were not many people over there, but then it's even evening. But I went in a room and had a blood line following me.

The same thing was I just remember one man and woman saying, "Oh my God, this man is bleeding badly. He needs help." That's what I remember.

But my car was parked in front of the hospital, and at that time I did not say to Csoko to follow me. I stepped out my car and closed the door and took myself to intensive care. They took care of my life and I lost a lot of blood and they gave me blood. So, in couple of hours I was talking to one nurse and a doctor and the first thing I said was "Thank you for helping me. I have a dog and I don't know what has happened." My dog was in my car.

She said, "Yes, we know," because I left a key in my car and somebody of course saw that a key was in my car. She said, "Move the car to a safe place," and my dog was in my car. I said, "Well, I have been in a hospital a couple times and the dog always stayed with me in the room. He's helped me a lot. Is it okay to bring him inside?"

The doctor said, "Certainly, if you want to bring in a dog."

I had pretty severe damage in my system. I stayed in the hospital nine days and then they let Csoko stay with me.

So, this was a little bit where I know not only how much my dog has done for a person but I have said he always looks like a dog, but he's a person because he does not bark when somebody goes by on a street or next to a car. He's an extremely nice and quiet person; earlier I mentioned that he's sleeping in his life at least about 95%. Mostly he's eating and takes a walk. That's something where he's not sleeping. Actually, while I'm talking about my story on an auto recorder, he's next to me here and still he's sleeping and snoring. I sit in a chair where there is a couch, but he's sleeping on his special bed. This dog is always and every day giving me happiness in my day.

Any place I go, and somebody has kids, he was extremely gentle with kids. Even when kids did some dangerous thing to walk on stairs or jumping around and he thought about it, that one was not very safe for kids, he stood up and almost he said, "Oh, look." He tried to make me pay attention. "Look at that, I hope these kids are not going to fall down and get hurt. She will hurt herself." So, she's an amazing person.

My daughter had her first child, and I held the baby in my hands. Whenever I went to my daughter or picked up my granddaughter, he came over and wanted to look at her, he would not lick her face. My daughter didn't mind when he came over and just put his nose by her face. He looked beautiful, and it always made for an extremely nice day and happiness. I mean it for everybody.

Today, I am staying in Alaska with my daughter. I have twin boy grandsons and my granddaughter. The twin boys are three years and eight months. My granddaughter is five years and eleven months. Every day has been extremely nice and he has made many, many nice, special days for me.

I drove a car all over the United States, and if he saw I was tired or hit a curb or run through something and he would stand up and check to be sure it's fine. A couple times I'd be a little tired and he thought about it that it's not safe for me to drive and he came over there and he'd be in the back seat. But he came over there and put his nose down and licked my ear and then also put his front legs on my arm. "You better be careful and pay attention to what you're doing."

So again, I have finished my chapter for my beautiful, special dog, Csoko. Please add on and finish that chapter also for my special dog. I love this dog, always. Everybody's dog is different in the world but that one is true.

Chapter 10

Immigration

I named this chapter "Immigration". It means somebody moves to the United States or any place in the world. They faced hardships because they didn't speak good English or came to a new country with nothing. They start making money and taking care of their families, especially those who have immigrated with children.

I am not saying only the United States, but any place in the world – Australia or Canada. Even somebody in one country had a dream to move to different places were two different people. It's about leaving a country. It's not even leaving their country. There can be a problem where the person does not have many skills but has a dream to go.

For example, now I will use the United States. In this country, I saw many nice movies on TV, especially soap operas, people were shown how nice life could be by going to Disneyland or other fancy things. Many people thought by coming to United States, they only needed to work a little and make lots of money. I will use these words: a lot of people said it's a green color, like a dollar. People were thinking about dollars growing on a tree. No, that one is not true. But I am telling you one thing. It's a world where one or two make it happen to start to a new life – number one in the United States.

Of course, in the United States there are also people waiting for new immigrants who don't speak English and then try to pay them a couple dollars. Or people start working barely a minimum wage, finished a job, and then don't pay them. Of course, some immigrants that come to the United States don't know what they are doing and then start to work and then before they finish a job, ask for money and get the money because they found a good-hearted person. This even happened to me. I am an immigrant, too. The new immigrants came here and I was able to start very well. I am a person who always likes to help other people, especially if somebody has a child.

Even when I was in Hungary, I always liked to learn more skills or start new things. I bought a book to make sure to follow the code, or I had a house plan and followed the directions on how to build a house and other things. I never liked to take a shortcut. I always did it the way I was supposed to do it. I picked up a job for myself or to help a family of new immigrants.

It doesn't matter what nationality. They just came here and needed work, and I was happy to do it.

In a short time, I had learned to speak English for materials. How I did it — as I already mentioned earlier in my book — I rebuilt engines for Star Motor. I put the parts in my language and then next to that I put it in the English language. I ordered them. Of course, I knew auto parts, mostly everything in my language, but I didn't know how I translated that to English. But it helped using a dictionary; the best dictionary for me was writing a word down in my own notebook in my language with the same line in English. It really did not matter if it was auto parts or building materials or anything.

I remember I picked up a job for myself. I mostly did it without a contractor license for everything. I did just have an auto repair license in the beginning, but I did not immediately have a contractor license because I was working really from friend to friend. I never advertised doing new construction. I did one kind of work for somebody – remodel a kitchen or a bathroom or tile a living room or anything.

I always made sure 99%, 100% of everyone liked what I did because, for example, I worked on something for ten hours but it took me ten hours to finish because I was stuck with a little problem. I knew I did a good job if there were no complications. It would take seven hours and then I only charged seven hours and not doing extra money.

Or somebody would bring a car to my shop and then I grew up with auto mechanics. I knew mostly I worked on Mercedes cars, but I fixed any car besides Mercedes. An engine was running and somebody explained it to me – or even when I did not speak much English, but somebody explained a bit – what was wrong with a car. Or they came over there and I heard how and the car was running and I heard how an engine was running. I knew the problem immediately.

I heard it with my ear it was really the engine or did it with a newer car – and OBD tester helped a lot. But with older cars I didn't use an OBD tester. The better way was definitely when I found out what the car owner was telling me, or I heard the engine and how it was running or drove the car around a block with the transmission and what it was doing or so many things because I was an expert at that.

Besides that, I did honest work on everybody's car. But sometimes it was somebody's friend. Somebody would recommend me to somebody else to work on his car. And then, for example, they would bring a car over there for a tune-up and check the car. I explained that, yes, on that car, it needed a tune-up done, but not just a tune-up. I think I already mentioned it earlier in my chapter that Mercedes cars had weak timing chains. As I mentioned, a person found that car had a noisy chain and it was possible for the chain to jump at any time and the engine would blow up or make big damage on an engine.

Even if I knew friend to friend in the auto repair business, I had for construction built up in my life. This was not just in the United States, but in Hungary also where I was working, of course, in one shop. Steve had a shop for many years. I learned a lot from him. I learned a lot from my father, too. I saw how he was doing in the agriculture business. My father had a tractor repair business and a little bit for cars, too. But he really made attention toward making money from farming.

But besides that — he did it but even just a little bit — my father took the product to a farmer's market and organized it and had a top-quality product for one price and then a little less quality product for less money. What he did not sell, he would not put that product in the garbage.

He took it to a farmer's market and then had people who liked to buy very nice vegetable products because they could afford it. Some people bought medium quality.

Somebody said, "Well, I will take this and not by how many kilograms or pounds."

My father said, "Okay, this basket of peach or grapes will be that price," and the person was happy to buy it because they didn't have very much money and still took home some kind of fruit or other food for their kids. That's all they could afford. He made it happen using all of the material and not putting it in the garbage.

I already mentioned it, he raised hogs and had a yearly customer come back many years. For ten to twenty years, this customer bought the hogs from him all the time. But he did not feed the hogs junk food. The hogs were supposed to be eating hay and vegetables and good food and he never did a shortcut, and I learned that from him.

I also worked in Steve's shop and saw he did not do shortcuts. He estimated to repair something and he did not say that even he knew extremely well how to estimate a car and find and figure out what was wrong with a car. But he never guessed. I was able to use these words about me, too. I used these words myself. I never said, , that car repair costs, for example, $500. And then because I ran judgment to find out what was wrong with a car and calling the owner, "Sorry, it will be another $500 because something else is wrong."

If I gave a bad judgment with a $500 estimate, even if I ordered the wrong parts because did not find out what was really wrong with the car, I did not double charge the owner.

But with a car and a building, I always gave good advice to people. I was not trying to tell someone I was the smartest person in the world, but I knew I was able to say that. I was well-educated and well-trained myself because, again, I bought a book. I came to the United States speaking zero English, and then somebody offered me a paint job. I had mentioned Steve, and I did the best for him for less money; I won somebody else. But I had to prove it. He had to know who I was and who this person they were dealing with to give him more work.

I already mentioned it: I came to this beautiful country in 1975 to make sure I was not making a mistake bringing my family here. Hungary is a beautiful country, but the communism damaged that country. Not only Hungary, but in Poland and many other countries — especially in Russia, or previously the Soviet Union.

But I'll tell you one thing, communism – in Hungary or Russia or Poland – was not exactly Marx and Engels what has been written that is communism. He did it because he wanted to help poor people to be more appreciated for what they were doing because there were a lot of rich people who really did bad things to poor people, like you read at the start of my mother's story. My mother started to work, lost her parents, and had no value. It didn't matter what she did. Even she had damage to her health and was not taken to a doctor. But she was not the only person for that. A lot of people had gotten damage from rich people.

In the world there are two types of people; many types, but I'm talking about two differences: working hard and doing an honest job and then he builds up appreciation and then he doesn't have a hard time to find another job. There is another type of people who give a price or work either way. It doesn't matter if it's estimated repair or working hourly and then go over there.

In communism, they would go over there at 8 o'clock or 6 o'clock. It didn't matter what time, if they started work in the morning or started the work and has a shift, an eight-hour shift and said, "Oh my God, okay. It's been great. I already spent one hour, two hours. Now, two more hours and I'm going home." But really, he didn't care what he did not make attention to or what he was doing.

As an example, in the United States, you go in a store and three salesmen run over to ask you what you want and how you want it. "Can I help you?"

In communism, people don't need to do it that because there is a monthly wage, not hourly. It's how much you make a month and pays twice, every two weeks. It does not matter if you did a good job or bad job or are working hard or not working hard. They don't care what you're doing, you get the same paycheck.

Over there, somebody said, "Oh, I'll take care of you very well," because that was the way I was raised. It did not matter. No appreciation. Nobody gave any attention; almost nothing is private. Everything is for the government. People learn fast to steal everything, even in Russia, Hungary, Czech Republic, and many other places.

But a government borrowed money from the World Bank to start a big...I'm talking about a billion-dollar project. But that one was really special in Russia, and they used the money to build weapons, not a factory. It's collective communism, not because it started the wrong idea, but because people were not honest and didn't want to give appreciation for what the government did for them.

My country has a lot of poor people and big families. And in places they have to work an extra day. It's not paid and then that money is used for poor people with six, seven children for a washer or put them in a nice apartment and there is no appreciation. They sold that washing machine. He didn't need a new washing machine. He didn't care. He sold it for nothing to rich people who were not honest. Many people were waiting to buy it for a brand-new item for nothing.

Because poor people, it's hard to say that but it's not that they don't know how they need to work to earn the money to buy this washing machine and he did not care about the value. It didn't matter he got the washing machine or got the $1000. It's equal. He spent the money in the wrong way.

I am not saying everybody did it, but a lot of people went that way or put it in a nice co-op or free apartment and the government paid the costs – even paid the electricity and everything — because the people had no education, no skills to do anything.

It's just hard to say that they were looking for a free lunch. Yes, they got the free lunch, but still there was no appreciation for more lunch, for a free lunch. I said it didn't matter if it was one penny or a hundred pennies, all the pennies need to think how they were spent and what they were supposed to buy for that money, not just buy one big thing. A lot of people bought a big TV, and then the kids didn't have a shirt, or other essential things because the money they got was spent on something else where they are not supposed to spend the money. It was a lot of money.

I went into politics a little, but I will return to immigrants and immigration. Here, in the United States, but also in Canada and many countries, people welcomed new immigrants. They made it happen too, yes, welcome them into the country. In this country, they gave them a Social

Security Number and didn't want people laying around and collecting a welfare check.

They had a possibility to go to a school to learn skills in their language. Kids had a great way to start a school – a special school in the first year – and a chance to go back one year to continue the school. For example, if somebody in their own country had second elementary and came back to start the first elementary over or went in a special program for one year, and then took the test at the end of the year, or even the middle of the year, they could make sure to keep him at the right class and not start one year back to continue to finish the education.

The immigration office was extremely helpful for everybody. Of course, it's the immigration office, and I'm saying anything new. If I said in the United States or Canada, a lot of people have come from around the world and built up this beautiful country, and then the government never took shortcuts for immigrants. Many immigrants did it by themselves because they did not follow it but supposed to follow it.

I already mentioned it. I did not make a mistake coming to this country. I came to this beautiful country and I was very happy to do it. But I made the mistake not going to an English class immediately because I didn't have anything. But the priority for me and my family was to get a job because I had one Hungarian friend and I spoke his language.

But after I made a little money, I made it a problem for myself. I did not hide I did not speak English, and finished school here. I don't know why I did not do it because, in my country, I finished school at an extremely, high level and I had two children who are extremely smart.

My daughter had a much easier time studying in a school, unlike my son. But I am not saying that because my daughter was smarter. There was some reason she knew what needed to be learned, and with less effort, she could memorize it better. One thing, I mean, she had an extremely good memory. I am not saying my son did not have a good memory, too, only different. But nobody is the same in this world. Everybody is different in one way or another.

I started knowing no English and had to prove to people I was the best. Not only that, but to finish a job nicely and to get back to a lot of people. Especially with kids, I needed help and I helped. I am not saying it came out 50/50. It only came out about 30% to have the appreciation and 70% with no appreciation. I got to the point where I was not disappointed. I helped somebody and made a hard time for me because I helped a bit.

I don't think I talked about it yet. There was one weekly magazine in Hungary I would get. I learned a lot, too. One man had a Ph.D. He wrote this magazine and two guys had a master's for public health. It was extremely good and I learned a lot from that.

I learned much from my father; he always ran a business to do things for others, but never for praise, such as, "I'm going to help this person because he's a very good plumber or electrician, and then I am going to learn from him. And then he will finish the job, and I don't care how I pay him."

No, I hired somebody to help me finish the job and watch him very carefully. Many times, I saw he did not really know what he was doing. Mostly, it came out fine to take my advice.

I said, "Hey, guys, I'm paying you. I saw what you're doing is not good. But I don't mind teaching you while I pay you. It cost me more. It will cost me time, and then I cannot do my job because I am teaching you how to finish the job. But I am not going to pay you less money. I'm going to pay you, but you have to do it my own way to finish the job."

I am not saying it was that way all the time. Again, sometimes somebody came to help me out and did the job, and then I would learn from them. I said, "Oh, wait a minute. I did it that way. Look how he does it. Next time, I am going to do it that way." I appreciated it.

A lot of people picked up a job that paid hourly and then that one – even I mentioned it –

it didn't matter if it's a minimum wage, and then I paid ten dollars. Not because I paid out cash. Because people had no bank, no checking, and then came in this country with almost nothing and had little help with welfare from the government or immigration office. But this was not the reason I paid him cash, because I wanted to cheat on the welfare department. It was what was happening to somebody in this country that had nothing and then money was needed immediately.

I tried to pay them with a check, because I had a checking account soon after I came to the United States. I had a hard time to get a driver's license. But they didn't have a driver's license because they could not afford to take the test or they did not speak enough English. The DMV could order that in any language for a test, and they let him take it in his own language. But still, a lot people were not ready to get a driver's license. For this reason, I paid the people money because I knew they wanted it; that way I made the people happier.

A number of problems happened if somebody came here, like a woman, but even if she came with a husband, but the husband – I don't know how I say that – did not really care about the family and then he made the wrong judgment to come in this country because he thought the work would be easier. Or he would be working a bit to make a lot of money and he would end up unhappy. He would not have the patience to learn way to need to work in this country.

Every country had codes and laws that were different. I told everybody to follow the rules in this country and not to worry about how nice the city and downtown was or if it was too hot, too cold. I said, "Number one is to find out which way you will be able to make good money, a higher wage." But the only way you will be able to get into higher money was if somebody did something very good to get a good paycheck. But a lot people, on that one, not just immigrants. Even somebody born here thought he knew very well how he needed to do it and didn't want to listen to the owner or follow the rules on how he needed to do it. I don't know how I can say that and still this many can't figure it out because they are lazy or hardheaded.

Another big problem for people was they made, for example, $10 per hour, and then he talked to somebody who said: "I am a carpenter or an auto mechanic and I make $15 an hour." They are getting $15 an hour because they had experience and he already earned $15 an hour because he trained himself and listened to the person who gave him a job.

It didn't matter if it's at a restaurant or cleaning somebody's house, they had to prove they were the best or would do their best.

My experience in the United States has been that I help people and there is appreciation. I told many people, "I will help you. Just one thing I would like to ask you to do for me as a favor. Don't give me a hard time or step in my marriage or my personal life."

Many immigrants came to the United States. As an example, my nephew lived in New York and he helped a lot of immigrants, too. He was working with a Greek contractor and he came here very young to the United States because he was only a seventeen-year-old. I helped him immigrate to the United States through Yugoslavia in 1974. He came here to this beautiful country and learned English very well because he's the only child that came to United States. He found that he was working hard to prove who he was and then started with his two hands, he worked. He was honest and a hardworking person. He'd work on with a Greek contractor. He was doing a lot of work in New York, especially in Manhattan.

I helped him to do many jobs, such as the Lincoln Center. We did an extremely big marble job and were paid a couple hundred thousand dollars. Both of them had come out pretty well because we wanted to prove we are the best. But he helped many immigrants to start their own lives, and a lot of them, not just a couple of them, went to a Greek contractor. He said a lot of them got paid $11 an hour, $9 an hour. It didn't matter. He thought about it. Well, he probably made $20 an hour for that much he would give them a Greek contractor.

So, he thought about it. He said, okay. He paid me ten dollars. This Greek contractor had a Hungarian wife and he didn't speak English at all, only Hungarian.

He did talk to a Greek contractor, "I will do this job for you for less money than Lazio or maybe you are paying him or he is working hard to finally paying him twenty dollars."

He said, "Just pay me fifteen and I'll do the job for you."

But this man didn't know because he was a new immigrant. He didn't know how a lot of materials worked because it was totally different than his own country and he didn't have the right information to how to use so many things. That one made a lot of hard times for my cousins and many other people. But it made a hard time for me to help people to straighten up their own lives.

With immigration, I think people were moving to one city because some-body said, "Oh, you will make a lot of money over there." People, of course, were not telling the truth because there were two friends together and then they would borrow money and spend the money to move to, for example, Se-attle or California. But in Seattle, house rent may be $450 and in California it's $900 because it's very nice.

And then it didn't matter. They made a little more money, but still did not make enough money to make a good life for a family. They would start to get disappointed and blame it on the United States or blame it to other people. But again, when was communism in his own country, he blamed it on com-munism. It was not that communism was not good. It was what he did by him-self that made a problem on his own.

In United States, just to stay in the United States, a lot of contractors were glad to hire immigrants. But again, a lot of them before they had fin-ished a job or even contractor or a company would try to teach him, and fi-nally they would know what they were doing. They didn't have patience or they were not going to give appreciation for that person who spent the time to teach them.

This had happened to me many times. I would teach and I help him do it and it cost me a lot of time, a lot of money. It would get to the point to know what he was doing and he did went or tried to open his own business or he went to work for somebody for more money.

But I will not say I am an angel and I'm the best person in the world. But still, he was not ready for this big change. A lot of people opened their own business without experience. It wasn't just me, anybody would help this person and he would even be able to save a little money to open his business but didn't have enough experience to learn the business and went in with a problem. Of course, he would blame the United States or Canada or Australia. It didn't matter. That could happen anywhere in the world.

It's very interesting what I will say now, but what I saw was extremely good, patient, and hardworking Portuguese and Mexican people. They were coming here working for very small wages and saved money and brought it home by working in the summer time and then going back to Mexico. I know

Western Union very well because I helped a lot of people send the money to Mexico or Portugal.

Portuguese people are here. There are some, but not like in New York. I even met Portuguese people because my nephew lived in New York and there are a lot of Portuguese in New York. In California, there are a lot of Mexicans. Many Mexican people have big families, but an extremely nice atmosphere and a simple life.

They were not dreaming of a big house. They wanted to make time to do it. Somebody who was working here and lived and working for very little money. And then they send it home to Mexico to help the whole family. It was very nice. I did not really notice that the Mexican people here were making money and bought a big boom box or spend the money for their own and go to do so many things.

But really, they had friends and working an old way. On Sunday, family would come together and help each together and not make people jealous. Other people gave advice, and when Mexican people were working for somebody, they try to keep their word and do the job. I did not say it's many other people where they were good and another was bad. I said I discover good things about people from different nations based on how hard they are working.

I am Hungarian, came here, and I was very happy to work with my fellow Hungarian people. But, again, it's unbelievable how much damage communism made of the people in Hungary because over there it was not necessary to work hard and still they got the money. They did not need it. Nobody cared what they were doing. They just got the check every two weeks and that's it.

Of course, it's communism. It didn't matter what was in the world. Somebody had a business and I was working for them, I had to do an honest job to continue for that person to keep his door open to running a business. I need to think about how I am doing to give him hard work — hard, honest work — to continue to work that man and help him to open his business door. But it's very sad in this world not many people think about it that way.

Here, of course, it's not that, I don't think so. I see many things new going into a Home Depot or Costco. At Costco, you don't need it. Mostly, you find everything. I just go back to Home Depot or Lowes looking for something.

Some people are walking around working there and really don't know anything. But a lot of them try to prove how hard they are working for that company to keep the doors open, and then make a buyer happy to be sure they will come back to the same store the next time to buying something to help find what it is they are looking for. It means to prove it, not just thinking about, "I am getting an hourly wage and then start 6:00 A.M. and go home 2:00 P.M."

But nobody is the same. Not everybody is thinking that way, but that this is a world where not everybody is the same and that problem is everywhere in the world. It does not matter where they came from. Not that it's a black people or white people or it does not matter.

Chapter 11

Separation

Here, in my marriage, I slowly have to step into a sad story, or part of a sad story. It happened like that. Here was the start of a problem earlier, but then I am an extremely strong Catholic. My family is a huge. No one had divorced because too much salt in a soup does not taste good in a lunch or a dinner. They would try to keep it to solve the problem and not divorce because they were thinking about going to the next relationship or marriage or – how do I say that – and then it would be getting better.

Again, I had a very strong love for my wife and my children. I already mentioned this earlier. In a marriage or a business partnership or just a friendship, people have to learn what is good for another person. In a business partnership, it is different. You split and start over. But, in my opinion, marriage today is not very easy. Even before, people need to work together and help each other together to make it work — everything day by day.

In the beginning, when I was married to my wife, I found a very interesting surprise. Even a year later, I found out we were totally different. I loved her strongly, but she had a difficult life as a kid. She handled everything. It was okay, but her parents divorced and she had problems with her brother. She didn't have any boyfriends, but I was the same. She was my second girlfriend in my life. In a very short time she had married. We only continued a nice marriage because, again, I loved her strongly. But she already, again I mentioned it, was nice to me, too, because there was no reason to change her mind. Because I don't think she even thought she would get something better.

It was a little harder in our life because we really had nothing. She was in school and I was already working and making money. But even my parents kept all the money I made. As I mentioned, I called Steve an adopted father because he and his wife really took care of me like a mother and father.

I accepted who my wife was and how she was doing. After she delivered me a beautiful daughter, and shortly after a beautiful son, I had two very nice children. I let her stay home and she did a nice job raising the kids. She didn't have any bad habits like smoking cigarettes or drinking alcohol at this time. My house didn't have alcohol because I never drank or smoked in my whole life.

As I mentioned, she was different from me, in that I grew up on a farm and she grew up in a city and was raised a different way. Her personality was different. She was raised to be really nice to me, but she didn't have a way to show that she loved me, just that she liked me.

Even at the beginning, I was thinking a bit that someday she would be so happy and stay with me because she had everything she wanted. She didn't know what she wanted. I read her mind and I bought it for her. Of course, again, in the beginning, I didn't have very much money. But I had flowers on the table all the time for her at least once a week and I knew what she liked.

I had an interesting childhood and was raised in an extremely difficult way, but I never even thought about it for how I was raised and what my parents did for me. That meant I accepted my parents and I loved them so much, very much, all the time in my life.

After she came into my life, I loved her deeply. I made it happen and gave her everything to make her happy. Again, I mentioned she felt different for the two children, and I accepted it even though I was not happy. But all the time I worked out how to do something to give more attention to our daughter. But really, I did not make it a daily problem for myself. I always worked to figure out how I was able to solve the problem to not go into a deeper problem.

Of course, she had a different life growing up in a city and liked to go more parties, but I didn't know how to enjoy going to parties because I had to work for my family every day. But even if I went to a birthday party or other festivity, I wouldn't know how because my parents never took me to a birthday party. Even if I went to a birthday party at my brother's house – when he was getting married or some relative's house – I always fixed a car or an antenna for a TV. At that time, it wasn't a TV. At first. I would just fix an antenna for a radio and fixed a bicycle and I always had something to do. Or I would play with a child, as this was the only time I would have a chance to play around the kids because in the home, again, I had to finish something all the time. I was not taught or didn't think about what was good or better or maybe if I was married to my first girlfriend. I already mentioned that her name was Julie. I took her out of my mind, but I never, ever watched another woman to see if she was nicer or better. Or why was she not the person that was my wife. I always accepted how she was.

In Hungary, she always had a friend and that was in another family where the wife was able to stay home. She came to my house and the kids spent a nice time with my kids. Even a couple of the children from these families liked me and thought I was extremely nice. But my nature was that older people or young children always liked me very much.

I had a lot of friends who would say, "How are you doing?" But I didn't have a part different.

I never went to a bar, as I mentioned; I didn't have the time and was never able to go to a barbeque because it affected my life. I needed to work all the time. I even had a hard time relaxing. Relaxation – after I got married and had a child – for me was to spend the time with my kids. Otherwise, I didn't even know how I needed to enjoy my life. The only way was with my family because that thing came in my heart which was the biggest change to marry her and then have two children. Even if we had a problem, she let me hug her and love her. This was the biggest gift she gave to me — of course, my two children, and that she stayed with me.

So, after many years, even Hungary had jealous people, as I mentioned, I did not look ugly and everybody said I looked nice. But she was an extremely nice lady.

As I mentioned earlier, there were always bad people chasing other women. They said, "Oh, it's Ferenc working all the time. I don't think he is able to take care of his wife, or if he coming home. How about you go some-place to enjoy your life." Of course, a lot of people were working hard trying to break my marriage. But I never found out the situation in Hungary. I was even not taught or thought about anyone able to get close to her.

But, in the United States, something had changed. People figured out that Ferenc was not doing anything and just working. But I was working very hard to change that. But I heard in my ear, "Don't sit down. Why don't you do that and that?" I thought about that I needed to do something. The sun had come up and I would start to do something. The sun went down, all the way till sun went down to do something.

Not just that, but in Hungary I started with nothing and had in my blood the need to work and make a bigger farm and make more money. I helped a lot of people because they needed help. I spent time giving advice. Money-wise, I would teach them how they needed to do something to make a little extra money.

I earlier mentioned that to buy a house or buy a car, many families could not dream or were never able to afford to buy a car or a co-op. Some bought a small house or a condominium. It depended. I helped many marriages happen by putting together the money because in these families the parents were very poor. They wanted to marry and could not even afford to rent a place or buy a wedding ring.

Then I let them come to my farm and if somebody was an auto mechanic, I had a shop and I picked up a job. I let him do it because I had so many things to do and then I could not handle them by myself. I paid the person very well. I need to mention that a lot of people were asking me for a loan. I said, "I love you so much and I like you and I don't want to lose a friendship. How about you come to my farm or my shop, work, and then I will be able to pay you very well," even if some people didn't have a very good skill or knowledge to do something. But I would say, "Come in and rake my yard on my farm or clean something. Wash my car or something." But I always did something to make somebody's life happy.

In the United States, what had happened was a lot of people immigrated to the United States, too. The sad part was from Hungary. It still did not have an open border but had a possibility to immigrate. A lot of people had come with two children to the United States and they had nothing. Even though they went to an immigration office and got everything mostly to help with an apartment. But they didn't speak English and didn't know how they to find work.

This didn't mean I spoke very good English because I was working and I had a hard time learning English. I made the mistake – if I think about it all the way to today – by not going to an English class. I was just working, working because I wanted to make a nice life for my family so fast.

What was sad was when an immigrant came from Hungary and then I helped. In a lot of places, I said, "Okay, I will pay you $10 an hour." And then minimum wage is $3-$4 an hour and I paid him $10 an hour because it didn't matter if a person spoke English or not since he spoke my language.

But many people found out — if they spoke English or not — and would open the newspaper, the Monterey Herald, and saw that a carpenter was making $15, $16 or $18 an hour.

The wife said or even the person said, "How come you paid me $10 per hour when a carpenter makes $16 per hour and somebody working in a restaurant gets $8 to $10 an hour?"

I said, "You have two children. I am still going to help you, but if you find a job $16 per hour, go ahead. Do it."

Of course, they were unable to do it because nobody would hire them. Even the Hungarian contractor I mentioned earlier – I called him Jimmy – would not hire them because he was sick and tired of this kind of people.

But again, that type of people, even they had a wife that was not a nice person, would try to get close to my wife or ruin my marriage. These people came from Hungary or I would help Romanian people from Romania or the Czech Republic and then they came from Portugal. Mostly, I helped people from different nations with their family.

And then from Hungary, not just a whole family came. Sometimes there would be men by themselves. I'm just going to mention one. He came from Hungary and really did not know very much and I tried to pick up a paint job. One time I picked up a paint job for a house because I thought about it. Everybody should know how to paint a house. But it was sad a lot of people didn't. They would just make a mess.

This man, I showed him: that paint is going to the fireplace, another paint for the wall and another paint for the ceiling. Of course, he messed up everything. So, I corrected it. At my cost, I bought the paint again. That was not my house. I just picked up a job for them.

What happened with this man was I bought the tools and everything and he said, "I found a pickup truck and I would really like to buy it."

I said, "I have a car here. Why do you need another car?"

He said, "Well, I met somebody. He's a Hungarian friend, but his wife is from Germany. He's a real estate person. He may be able to find me job, but I need a pickup truck."

I bought him a small truck for $1700 that needed a little work, and then I fixed it. I helped him go to the DMV and work on insurance and everything. Of course, I came up with the money and he said, "Well, can I have a skill saw?" I had a couple skill saws there. I wanted to give it to him. He said, "Oh, I always like new tools because I am going to take care of them."

I said, "Look at it. It's almost brand new." So, I bought a new skill saw, jigsaw, and chop saw for him. I spent about hundred-some dollars.

In Carmel, I picked up one job. The owner was also Hungarian. It was a Hungarian Jewish family; his wife was from Israel and the man was from Hungary. He had a house in Carmel and had a shoe repair store, selling shoes, and repairing shoes on Saturday. I showed him what he needed to do and he came by on Saturday. He came with one woman and the woman had two children. And, of course, she didn't speak English.

He stayed in another Hungarian's studio. He said, "Well, I would like to move into a house."

As I mentioned earlier, Father Doman — who I was going to talk to on the phone — he was a Catholic priest, and his last name is Doman. For this reason, I called him Father Doman. He helped me a lot and I met him in the beginning when I went to Monterey. I came to the Oratorian. An Oratorian is a very small main office in England. But it's for Catholic priests to live in Monterey.

They had a house that somebody donated to them. I fixed the house for this man that said he was going to get married to whatever and they are living together like a family.

I said, "Okay, I will help you guys." It didn't matter how busy I was. I went again to buy the paint, clean the house, and then it had a hole over there for a dishwasher.

He said, "Oh, that would make me so happy for my girlfriend to get a dishwasher."

I was very good at finding on a street or going to a place to buy a dishwasher extremely cheap or free. I got the dishwasher and put that in.

He said, "Well, how about — because I have two kids – a washing machine?"

I got a used washing machine and a used dryer, but it worked fine. I fixed it if it did not work fine because I learned in Hungary to repair washers and dryers. Dryers weren't actually in Hungary, but a dryer was not really complicated to repair. It was a heating element or the belt was broken. Mostly that's all the problem was. There were many places where you just need to go over there to pick it up. Monterey had a section where it is free. At that time, I was not messing a rental store or eBay or anything, just Monterey Herald.

I fixed everything, but this bad person tried to mess around with my wife. But she, of course, did not accept it and just told me. And even because of the two kids, I just closed my eyes. I said okay. I just left it. So, he started the work on this Carmel job. It's a pretty big job in Carmel and inside. I stepped in more and bigger jobs. In that house somebody had put in wallpaper before on the house and repainted it. And these people want to take out the wallpaper, so I knew very well that one, too. I had the tools, the steamer to take out the wallpaper.

I showed it to him, but he owed money. It was hard to follow how much money he owed me — for a car, tools, and so many things. Even Father Doman let him put no money down for rent on the first month, last month. I paid the first month's rent and he did let him pass on having him pay the rent for the second month. He was supposed to pay the last month and then the second month, the first month and last month. So, everybody helped him or tried to help him.

One time, he came over there on a Friday afternoon. He said, "It's Friday. I don't care if you got the check or not. I need some money."

I said, "The person that owns the house has not paid me one dime yet because you not work very much. But how much money do you need?"

He said, "Fifteen hundred dollars."

I said, "Fifteen hundred dollars? For what?"

He said, "Well, we want to find a couch."

I thought, *Wait a minute. This guy is not telling me the truth. Something is wrong here.* I said, "Well, I have money. But I don't think I am going to give you $1500."

He said, "Give me $1000."

I said, "For what? Do you need food? I will go with you to a store and buy food. But you have some furniture in your house. You have a bed to sleep on and I brought a kid's bed, food, and shirts, and more than you need."

This guy came back in a couple hours. He was so upset, he left for a couple hours, came back, and said, "Okay, give me $800."

I said, "No." He spit at me and almost kicked me. I said, "Oh my God. What is wrong with you?"

This became a serious problem and I called Father Doman. I didn't have an clue what I should do with this man. He's seriously forcing me to give him money.

He said, "Well, Ferenc, I was just going to call you. He just left and I gave him $1000," because he lied to him saying he did all kinds of work and he missed me or whatever. He badly needed the money. So, the Oratorian and gave it to him.

Even I didn't know at this time, but he had a checking account; he seriously wanted money. This bad guy bothered Father Doman and gave him sometime before 5 o'clock $1000. And somebody said that at midnight he left. He took the truck. He took all the tools. He left this girl with the two kids and he just disappeared.

I saw that this woman was a hardworking mother. I asked her where she came from and everything. She just told me in Seattle, Washington her husband left her over there and then went with another woman to Canada.

I said, "All right. My God, I don't know how you are going to make it." But I do not want to go into details.

I helped this family a lot for the two children, but only I did not do anything else. I just helped this family and never touched or got too close to this woman.

In Monterey, I knew one Italian person. He was a very wealthy person with a Mercedes, Jaguar. I think he also had a Rolls Royce and a PhD as a business professor. It had always been my wife's dream to have a friend and "Oh, he has a PhD." This person gave me a hard time in my life.

He had a big job for his house. Again, I helped a Portuguese family and because I was pretty good at rebuilding engines and transmissions and a house I did not have to step into more construction. But, one way or another, I was involved in construction for a couple reasons. I made some money, but I did not do it for money. I liked to do it. I loved to do the construction. But the main thing was to help another person, teach them and do it together because that family or person did not speak English and I had to help.

I learned to speak Mexican and Portuguese. I could use it and to speak to both people and also there was a Hungarian man. He was a pretty nice man and had a Polish wife. There was another one from the Czech Republic. I made it happen — one way or another way — to have no miscommunication. I showed them what needed to be done. If people wanted to make a little money, it did not really matter if they spoke English or not if they showed them how they needed to do it or what needed to be done.

I always made it happen. Even the immigration office in Seaside next to Monterey had my telephone number and my name. When a new immigrant family came, they just called me. Of course, at the Oratorian, Father Doman helped a lot, too, for poor people to be together.

And then, this man said he had an Italian villa and he needed me to do a big job. I had a bad feeling. I did not really want to do it. But again, I had people who needed to earn money to have food and pay the rent. I said, "Well, I'm going to take that job, too." I needed to build a new deck and then new tile in the bathroom. But that house had probably 7000-8000 square feet.

This man was from Italy. He was actually born in Sicily. He went to visit and then said, "Well, I always dreamed of going to Hungary."

And it's very sad. He waited for the end of school. He was a business professor, but also a teacher in Monterey – in the Navy Postgrad or something like that. He taught over there as a business professor.

This man figured out my wife was going to Hungary and he went at the same time. But, I was working on his house and I did not say anything. I did not have any bad feelings and then I was unable to go to Hungary because I continued to rebuild engines and transmissions or into house remodeling or something, so I couldn't make it back to Hungary.

I mentioned it in my chapter earlier, I enjoyed every single day and hour in the United States because I love this country very much. All the way to today and again, I always said I am on vacation in this country, and somebody on vacation just enjoyed it day by day. I was happy to stay here, too. There was no reason to go back to my country because I had a family over there and if somebody wanted to see me or meet me, I bought the ticket and they came to the United States.

But, my family would go back to Hungary every summer for at least two and a half months. I never thought about how much it cos. I was so happy to do it.

So, at the time, this man went. I did not know he would be going the same day and follow my wife. What happened during this time, I really, up to today, don't want to know.

It wasn't just that summer. It was a couple times she was in Hungary that my relatives saw she was in a restaurant with another man. I just went to a church and I asked God to help me through this terrible news. I looked at my two children as nobody else was going to raise these two children. I would do it. I was not going to divorce my wife because somebody stepped in, as I called it, a beautiful marriage because I made it beautiful. I worked very hard and even I was not taught to make a divorce happen.

So, this man and my family were in Italy and Hungary for the whole summer or two months. Then, this guy came back and I spent close to $20,000 on his house. And again, earlier I mentioned in my book, there was a lumber yard called M&S Lumber Yard. I picked up lumber over there and did his fence. I did everything on this house. but again, not because I needed a job for me that way. It was extra work.

I did not call the extra work actually as a headache, but I enjoy it. It was my heart. It made me so happy to see I helped another family and always my heart was so happy to see it. Even a family came over there, little child or wife or husband all together, would hug me. Many times, a husband and wife would hold my hand and pet my hand and said, "Ferenc, you have a bold heart. You are an extremely nice person."

I am not trying to say I am an angel and the only person in the world that has talent. Even somebody who didn't believe in God, but because I was raised like a Catholic and I learned that way in my life I believe very strongly in God. I said you guys are lucky because God sent you here to find the right person to help you to continue your life in this beautiful country.

This guy came back and he had not paid for the lumber and the labor for what I did on his house. A sad part again was even after he had not paid me, he came to my house to visit my wife. It's hard to believe it, but I saw he was coming in my house. I did not go home. I just drove by and went back to the shop and slept in the car. That one was more serious and I just continued to love my wife so much.

I will never forget it. It was on April 24th. At that time, we were married for twenty-five years. I bought her fresh flowers to put on the table all the time. I went to a store. I didn't know what I needed in a store for myself, but I knew what I needed for my daughter, my son, and for her, what her favorite food was, what favorite toy was for my son.

I was never crazy to buy a bunch of toys. But later, my daughter had a Nintendo which my son and daughter liked. It made me happy to see my family was happy and we had food on the table. I ate what was my family favorites and also my favorite too because I didn't have different tastes. I liked the way she liked it and how my family liked it. I saw my family was happy because we had on the table what they want and already it's for me gave me big happiness in my heart.

That one man gave me a really hard time and he continued to do it. Earlier as I also mentioned was Fisherman's Grotto and my son and my daughter went over there to sell flowers for this man. They sold roses; either six or just one. They did not sell a dozen. It was half a dozen or just one to make a little money.

Not because my children didn't have money. I wanted to teach them. I already mentioned it in my children's chapter. I taught my children to work and how they needed to do something to earn money.

That place did not cost extra time for me because my wife would take our children over there. But she started to dress very sexy over there. I did not say anything because I did not know why she did it or that I didn't like for her to do it. I did not go on that point. I said it's okay. She wanted to dress like that. Okay, dress like that. I just didn't want to start a fight in my house. I never wanted my child to see any fights or disappointments.

Then my daughter said a couple of times, "Mommy, what kind of shirt is that? Everybody can see what you have under your shirt."

She would just laugh and then she didn't take time to park the car in a different place. She sometimes had a parking ticket for a couple hundred dollars over there in Fisherman's Wharf because they didn't have many parking spots and needed to move the car every two hours.

But again, I said it's okay and I did not say anything. I was still working a lot of hours and started to have a hard time handling this sad thing to see that. So more I did not go home. I stayed and slept in the shop. I stayed home and checked on my children to make sure everything was fine. I would say, "I'm sorry. I need to go back to work." I went to my shop because I didn't like to see what was going on in my house.

I was thinking a lot about how I solve this problem. I tried it one way, another way, and another way. I said, "Well, okay, I know how I'm going to do it." I had a house in a nice neighborhood. And I said, "I'm going to fix and sell that house."

When I started life in in northern California, I thought I would move back to Redding, California. My son went to firefighter school in Redding, California, and then I looked at the real estate. In Monterey County, actually that name has a subdivision and over there one lot was $318,000. I figured out northern California in Redding one lot was $37,000. It had two lots over there and I had cash.

AI said, "Well, I'm going to buy the 11 and 12 lot like a cul-de-sac. It had an extremely nice view to Mount Shasta. It had a very nice view and it had secluded gate and everything very nice — subdivision, clubhouse, and swimming pool. I said, "Okay, that's something I need for my family."

At that time, my daughter was already in Los Angeles at UCLA in her second year, and my son started his first year of firefighter school. I bought the lot in northern California, Redding. I knew very well how I need to do a house plan. I learned it in Hungary. Slowly, I made a house plan with about 2672 square feet – three bedrooms, three full bathrooms, a huge dining area, a family room in the downstairs, and the upstairs had a huge master bedroom and two walk-in closets and separate toilet and double showerhead.

I made the house plan and still I had a problem with English. I hired somebody to write in English what needed to be done. Because I did a huge roof system and in San Jose, somebody did an engineering roof system. I decided to go to building a house in northern California. In Redding, I thought about whether it would change and see if I was able to save my marriage.

My wife's cousin was still living in Redding, California. But, at that time, her cousin was divorced from her husband. And then I will never forget. So, in Monterey I did not sell it, but let him to step in my auto repair business. He came up with some money to start a business, but I did not sell that to him completely.

I said, "In the future, I'm going to sell it to you, but, at this time, just step in with some money if you are serious."

He came over and I was so busy. I already mentioned I hired so many workers to help me finish the auto repair because I wanted to do construction. So, he continued to work at the Mercedes shop I had renting in Monterey.

Redding had one half acre. It was not a nice neighborhood. A lot of homeless people were all around, but I put it in God's hands to buy that place over there that had almost 4000 square feet building. I had an auto repair shop over there, and mostly what I did was rebuild engines or transmissions.

This man brought it up to me to Redding and then over there I found somebody to help me to work on auto repair business because I was building an extremely nice house. And at that time, one cousin came from Hungary and helped me to build that house. And then also I hired people, not as a contractor but just workers to work on a house because the house was on a hill and there was a time constraint to building the foundation to do it to like owner builder.

I will never forget. I finished the foundation and everything. The framing for the first floor had been started. I always had good communication with my wife's cousin. Her divorced husband came over. They were not fighting, and sometimes they went to a store together. But one late afternoon, almost evening, they came over to my place and saw the nice view and the big house I was going to build. It was very interesting; this was the last day they came to visit me before they quit our friendship. They never returned to look at what I was doing. I thought, *Okay. No problem.*

But that was no problem, but I had another problem. Before, her husband was a very good friend. He would talk to me, and also had one brother who lived in San Leandro, California. He was another family troublemaker, but he talked to me. Then his brother said different things to me and my wife.

I said, "You know what, guys? Don't call me. Don't talk to me. This is what you're doing."

So, the problem continued over there. Not for me. She found a person doing something they weren't supposed to be nice to the family.

What had happened in 2002, I did not listen to many things in music, but Monday evening had a radio channel from Utah. One Mormon preacher was always talking, and somebody called in about a marriage problem. I listened to this channel a lot on Monday evenings from 6:00 to 7:00. One man called and explained almost the same situation and problem that I had. He had separated from his spouse and then gave it to God.

In 2002, my wife and kids went to Hungary. At this time, my daughter did not go. She was busy doing summer work, and my son and wife went to Hungary. I rented a beautiful condominium with two bedrooms and a one car garage. It was very nice, and then I bought her a white Mercedes.

She went back to Hungary, visiting Italy and all over Europe along the way. My son mostly stayed in Hungary from what I know. So, when she came back and I said, "Well, I made it easier for you to do anything you want in your life, so you cannot embarrass me or make me sad." I filed for separation on September 2, 2002. I filed it before she came home on September 4th.. "I want you to look at it. This is a new place you're going to live." I said, "The house is finished, and then I'm going to sell the house and give you money."

So, I did work on that house. I moved her in nicely, and I will never forget.

It was a nice, white Mercedes, but she said, "That car is just like an ambulance car," because in Hungary the ambulance was white. She did not say it was a beautiful Mercedes. It was a C220, a 1996 Mercedes. That happened in 2002, but it was not a brand-new one, but very nice. Of course, it needed a little work, so I fixed it. I always liked to do it like that.

I moved her in; it was a big surprise to her. I worked on the house I was building.

My niece who lived in New York had a man do a job there. It was winter and my niece said she had a man who seemed to be a nice person. But, I will mention that while we were on the phone, he found out I lived in California.

He said, "Well, I don't have a place. I don't have many things. Can I have his number and talk to him? I'm going to California and then I can work at his place, even if he doesn't have a lot of work. Just let me stay." He even figured out I had a shop. "I can sleep in a car."

My niece gave him my number and he called me and explained, "Just please let me go to California." Then this man was here crying. At that time, I bought the ticket for him because somebody owed him. He got the ticket to come to the San Francisco airport while I was going from Redding to deliver parts. There was a business to go down to Redwood City and also down all the way to Monterey.

He came around 4:00 P.M., and then he came out. There was traffic, so I did not make it over there to wait for him to come through to check his baggage. He was already waiting for me. I drove in front of Pan Am Airlines. And then I saw him. I said, "Wait. Please don't come out. Stay here." I said, "I don't want you to stay in California. I have to go to Redwood City and I'll be back to send you back to New York."

He said, "No, no, no. Please, please. At least let me go with you and talk to you."

I said, "Well, okay. I am already late because of the traffic, so please sit in the car and then I will talk to you."

He put his hands together and prayed, "Please, please, please. I believe in God and I am a nice person."

I let him go with me, so we went to Redwood City. He was able to change my mind. I picked up the luggage and took it. I took him to my shop.

Over there, he worked. He came to the shop and then he said, "Oh, I know that."

I said, "Okay. Go ahead and change the brake pad on that car."

Of course, he didn't know how to do it. Okay, another car needed the alternator to be changed. Of course, he didn't know how to do it.

I said, "Oh no, now what?" I said, "Okay, just wash the car."

He, of course smoked his cigarettes; he smoked two packs a day. I forgot to say that even as he left the San Francisco airport and he said, "Please, stop in the next 7-11 and buy a case or carton of Marlboros for me."

Well, for some reason, life wanted me to do that stupid thing, so I did.

I found out this man was worthless; he said he knew how to lay bricks very well. I knew a lot of people. I said, "Okay, I will find a job for you to do bricklaying."

And then, I picked up a job that was bricklaying. He did okay. I didn't mean it was perfect, but the man said it was okay. I didn't mean so happy, but fine, he did it. It's okay, because he did it much cheaper than somebody else. So, he did bricklaying.

This man gave me a $500 check. So, of course, he knew and was checking up on the money. I cashed the check and gave him the money. In my shop, there was a studio. I lived in the studio, but I also had a motor home where somebody brought a Mercedes for me to work on and then traded it for the labor. He gave me a pretty nice motor home.

After he came here, he did not need to live in a car because I had this motor home. Before, I did not use it to live in, but I made it happen to connect the water and everything. I had the water and even found a sewer line for that property. I connected the motor home and even made it legal with the city because it was a place that couldn't do very much without a permit because the city officials would drive by the front of the shop almost daily. I thought, well, anyway if they found out there was somebody living in the motor home, I'm going to get into problems. I did everything in order and legally.

What happened was he got a little money and I saw it. I mentioned the shop was not too far from a homeless shelter. I saw that he brought a woman over, and I was not happy. It was happening around Friday evening. On Saturday, he brought another woman over there.

I thought, *Oh no. Now what is going on?*

Another friend was already talking about putting a little tile in a shower and because he said he knew how to do it, I took him over there and he started to put tile in the shower. And then the owner called me around noon — around 2 o'clock, 3 o'clock or something like that. "Ferenc, please come over here. I have a problem."

I said, "What?"

He said, "Number one, he is smoking in the house."

That one was a new house actually. Somebody built a new house and it needed tile work. He said he was doing the tile work. So, I went over there. I saw what he was doing and that was bad. I brought him back to the shop.

Actually, it's interesting. His name was Ferenc, too. I said, "Hey, Ferenc, there is a problem. You need to go back to New York or somewhere else. You can't stay here anymore." I don't know what was wrong with me.

He said, "I already helped you here and cleaned that, and clean that."

I had a Mercedes, a 560SEL. It just needed a little paint job.

He said, "Can I have this car?"

I said, "What are you talking about? You want that car?"

He said, "Yes."

I said, "Okay. Here is a car."

He left some $114, and I gave him another $500. Yes, I'm not lying. But I had a bad feeling. This happened over a couple months. It was back and forth for about three or four months. I didn't know he was already messing around on my wife.

I gave him a car and money, went to the DMV to release the car from my name to his. He left the shop. I gave him the directions on the Highway 80. I almost said to drive day and night. Drive 80, 8-0, and go to New York. At that time, the gas was only about around eighty-eight cents and ninety cents, too. It was easy to make it with $500 to New York, plus he had $114 to $600.

I said it was fine, but I already lived separate from my wife. I was renting a place over there. I paid the rent for my wife's place. For some reason, I did not make it over for at least a month, or month and a half. But the guy that cut the grass in the backyard and the front, he wanted to show it to me. The real estate property management called and told me somebody built a gazebo in the backyard, and it's not legal. The backyard had a portable swimming pool.

I said, "What the hell are you talking about? Are you kidding me or what?" I went over there one morning around 9 o'clock. I had an appointment with this guy. I just look at it. I thought, *My God, how come there is this blue 560SEL Mercedes?* It was parked in front of the condominium. I put it together in my mind, and I said, "God help me for showing this person what I needed to do. Look at what is going on in the backyard." I saw the gazebo and portable swimming pool and everything. It wasn't that I was nosey, but I saw this in the backyard. It had a little courtyard. It had a pretty good-sized backyard, plus it had a little courtyard. I stepped in the courtyard and the master bedroom area and the screen door was closed. But the door and the curtain were not pulled, and my wife and that man were together in a bed. Of course, I did a separation. It was her right to do it. It was fine, but I didn't have a girlfriend because I didn't want my girlfriend telling me what I needed to do for my children.

I will stop for now and then I'm going to continue this sad thing.

Chapter 12

Divorce

My wife had a negative comment, or she said, "I'm always going to protect my own country, Hungary." Finally, in the middle of June, 1986, there was a chance where the whole family could go back for the first time to Hungary with my two kids, and she had already gotten a permit. At this time, we were not citizens yet.

But, honestly, I thought about how much she said: "I like Hungary and that place is much better." She was going over there with our two children and she was not going to come back to United States. Not just because she was always talking about how nice Hungary was and how much she didn't like it in the United States. I had thought about that she was not coming back.

She took a lot of money and brought so many things to Hungary. I didn't have a chance to do anything. It was okay, and I had to stay in United States because I always had a lot of things to do. I was always involved at some kind of job. I was not interested at all to return to Hungary because I like it very much in the United States.

They left in the middle of June, and I knew they were coming back August 28th, just a couple of days before starting school. I waited first with less than one week before August 28th. It was very hard for me because I was sure I had a feeling I was going to lose my two children in United States and they were not coming back to this beautiful country.

At that time, I didn't have a cell phone, but I had a phone in my house. The last couple days before August 28th, I was not working because I was waiting at home for the phone to ring to say they're coming to San Francisco airport. I had an answering machine, but if there was something wrong with the answering machine, I didn't want to miss a phone call. But she was not calling with the exact time they were returning from Hungary.

But, thank God, she called me on August 27th to say everybody was coming home, and that visiting Hungary caused a big change. She was not homesick anymore. Not just her, but anybody who stayed in United States two or three years. Anybody who stayed a half year realized how much better it was to live in this country. I always said somebody who had not lived in another country didn't know the difference, and how lucky they were to be in this beautiful place on Earth. Of course, the United States had some problems; everywhere had nice days or hard days. But, still it was for our age or middle of people, either way, this was the best place on Earth to live.

Finally, they came back and, thanks to God, she changed a bit. But still when there was anything to do with a party, I did not go because she had different comments. I also had a lot of customers and she started calling my customers.

She was not working and I never forced her to go to work. She never got a hairdressing license in the United States. She mostly stayed home and liked to sleep in till about 11:00 A.M. Slowly, she started to act a different way that controlled her life. I decided I was not going to say anything, because I found out if I said something, I was just going to be misunderstood, so I figured it was better I just talk about necessary things.

She started to give me a hard time about why I was not watching TV and I was reading. I always liked to read a lot of magazines, even magazines that came from Hungary, or a New York Hungarian newspaper and a California Hungarian newspaper. These two newspapers had an article and I always liked to read it. I was interested as I liked to talk about the politics. But, many times, they had articles I liked very much.

So, then what had happened was a job that I did. She got a phone number and called my customer. Anything my half-sister sent to me from Hungary, she hid it the mail, or even opened the mail, and she would have a criticism.

She always had a bad comment for my relatives when they sent me any mail. I had to call back anybody who sent me anything from Hungary. It was every year, they would go back to visit Hungary and somebody sent me something from Hungary. It would be food that was eaten on the way here, or she left it home and would not bring it to me.

I am not saying I am an angel. But I know I did not change anything to continue the marriage like before. I was always working hard to find out how I could make her happy and make a peaceful, nice marriage.

One day, she started dreaming she was so beautiful and deserved a nice husband who had a Ph.D. She craved a person with a Ph.D. But more and more it came up, and she was more vocal about how I was doing everything wrong because I was not going to parties. I was not watching TV. Just reading a newspaper and going to sleep. But I worked by myself and never knew how to enjoy parties. I did not drink alcohol. It was very sad. There were very few parties that didn't serve alcohol. I had my customers and, of course, I had some friends. I did go to my friend's birthday party, but she dressed very sexy and some friends didn't like that, especially my wife didn't like how she was dressing. Also, I was starting to talk about some politics or some article for my friend or my friend's friend at the party. She stopped me and said, "No, Ferenc grew up on a farm."

She didn't know what he was talking about or if somebody asking me something from Hungary. I always said, "Hungary is a beautiful country, but communism extremely damaged it."

And there were people who didn't need to know how to work hard anymore, because in 1956 a lot of Hungarians came to New York, Pennsylvania, an all over the East Coast. By nature, Hungarian people were very hard-working and knew so many skills. Even today, somebody who knew I was Hungarian and said, "Well, Hungarian people are very hard-working people."

I said, "Not anymore. It's a new generation who grew up in communism. They don't know what responsibility is or what they need to do and quit working to keep a job." Actually, I do not mean "keep a job" because it doesn't matter what a person did under communism. They did not really care very much about what they were doing because nobody cared what was going on since everything was owned by the government. Everybody was just thinking about how they could steal something and take it home, or just every day go over there to start the work and had a big break and said thanks God. Today is finished and go home. And then people forget how they need to work hard.

Not everybody. They were still had some private businesses because it had communism. The government in Hungary allowed some private business. Even I had a private business. I had a farm. But many people were not really interested in working hard. Because, like in United States or Germany or many other countries that have private businesses, somebody really needed to know what they were doing or working hard because, otherwise, they were losing a job and needed to prove it. In Hungary, a person didn't have a resume to show for how much experience they had. In Hungary, when I had different skill, I was hired to auto mechanic work and didn't know what I was doing. But people were not interested to know if he was good mechanic or not.

I just mentioned Hungary because I always received negative comments. As an example: I did a Ford engine for somebody. But this man was a psychologist and had a Ph.D. Actually, I did an engine for his brother. He had an auto mechanic shop in Los Angeles. I did an engine for him, a diesel engine to rebuild it. He called me and said, "Frank, is our engine done?"

I said, "Of course. I told you it would be done in the middle of the month, on the 15th. Even before the 10th, I finished the engine." I finish about seven or eight a month. That was not very much.

He said, "Where are you now?"

I said, "Well, I am not at home because I'm in North California, Redding; I have another shop. The next couple of days I am in Redding because I have an appointment with another customer." I always drove up to northern California. I stayed over there to finish a car repair for a steady customer, and then I went back to Monterey. At that time, I stayed three days in norther California. The third day, I went back to Monterey.

I just had a surprise. The Ford engine was not there and then the first surprise was the garage door was open. Say what? How come the garage door was open? I went inside and saw my toolbox was missing, the Ford engine was gone, and the engine hoist was gone. I just couldn't believe it.

I asked my wife, "What has happened? Did this guy come here and take the engine or what?"

She said, "Yes, I opened a door because a man said he paid for the engine. Everything was paid and he picked it up."

I said, "No, this guy did not pay for the engine. You know I never pick up money upfront. Everybody always pays me when a job is done."

For some reason, I used to do it in Hungary. I knew it when somebody ordered something and when it was finished and then they paid it. I always kept this system. To this day, if I am doing a job, once it's done, then I take the money.

So, then a said to her, "The garage door is a little open and my toolbox is gone and so many other things are missing in the shop." I said, "You went with him, too?" She explained to me that this man had a Ph.D. and it was probably his brother. She really didn't want to know who the other guy was, the brother or a friend or whatever.

She said, "I just gave them a key and they picked it up."

It's very sad. I found out, because next to my shop was a Burger Barn or it's on a corner and not exactly next to it. It's just down the street on a corner about 500 feet. But anybody who came to my shop drove in front of this Burger Barn. The man who owned the Burger Barn was an extremely good friend. He said, "No, Frank. I saw the guy had come over and opened the gate and your shop." He said he thought about it, "Who is this guy who's going into your shop?" He said a little later he came back with a U-Haul truck and stayed over there for a couple hours, and then he was gone. He said he saw the gate was open and the garage door was open, but he just couldn't believe what was going on. It was one afternoon and the whole night, all the way to the next morning, the gate and the garage door was open.

One thing that was very sad was I was unable to prove he took the engine without paying for it or that he took my toolbox. He said he already paid me. And even then, I almost had a problem because he said, anything I did for him, he paid me cash. I never liked that because I always gave a receipt for everybody. Either way, I had a license, an auto repair license, and I didn't want to get in trouble. But also, not number one but I thought about selling the shop and having a nice record of how much money I made for myself. So, in that way, it was a big loss.

Earlier in my book, I mentioned that one Pakistan man called in Monterey, Fisherman's Grotto. He had a restaurant on Fisherman's Grotto in a fisherman's wharf. My wife went over there to spend time in the afternoon at the restaurant, and I just closed my eyes and said nothing.

She went to a teriyaki and she never offered to take me, but I was never interested. Even if she offered, she knew I would not say anything bad. But she was not asking me if it was okay going to teriyaki and so many things. So, slowly she changed.

I said, "Well, it's okay."

My daughter got to the point of finishing high school in Monterey and started school in Los Angeles. I helped her a lot financially and helped her start school in a dorm. But, she was unable to study in a dorm because she said many people were going to sleep at midnight or 2 o'clock in the morning. They had parties and she was not used to it.

She was not a person to be going to a party. She was always going to sleep at ten at the latest She went to sleep because she worked very hard and did volunteer work in a nursing home and at a hospital. She always made herself busy. Too tired to stay up late, she was not really interested much to watch TV.

It happened more and more that my wife said a man was watching her because she was so cute, and then we came to an anniversary. I bought a flower.

She said, "Why did you buy a flower? I never want to remember this is the day our marriage happened."

I said, "Well, someday is coming when you're going to like to be married."

My son was home at that time. I thought that we probably needed change and should move back to northern California, Redding and have a new place, and it wouldn't a problem. I had people coming to my house and I was not happy to see them. Northern California had one subdivision, a lot for sale. I bought just one lot. It was $36,000. Another one was $37,000. I bought the two lots for another $100,000; in Monterey one lot is around $300,000 or

$318,000, something like that. I said it didn't matter. I lived in Monterey County. Nice, very nice in Monterey, but very expensive. I decided to go up to northern California.

I already had one small shop over there and a customer, and I knew that I had all the customers in San Jose, in the Bay area, all over. If I wanted to continue to work in Monterey, I said I was going back to finish the job. It was still possible to specialize in a big job rebuilding transmissions and engines. I decided I'd pick up a job and I take it up to Redding and do that over there. I knew I would be very busy in Redding building a house. Before, I made one house by myself. I thought about that someday I would build a house where I could retire and going to live in that house. I did build. A house plan was finished, but somebody wrote on a paper the measurements and for English what was needed to put it on a plan. Also, in San Jose, one engineer did the roof engineering. So, then I start to building house like an owner/builder.

I sold the house in Monterey so I would not have more property in Monterey. I tried to keep a shop open in Monterey and then I found out it was too much time to go back and forth and not necessary. I knew I had a big project I needed to finish because the house was almost 2700 square feet with three bedrooms and three bathrooms. The lot was on a hill. I had to do a lot of work to cut a lot of trees out and make it to happen to be able to start to build a house. That one happened in the fall of 1991.

I started building a house and it was a very interesting house. It was at that time I started building a house that one relative came from Hungary to help me to build it. All through the winter, there was a lot of rain in Redding. But, at that time, it was almost day and night that it was raining. I just bought the raincoat and he and I built the house and all the time it was raining.

I was a very well-organized person. I always kept everything so nice. I finished the foundation and then at that time her cousin was already divorced from her husband. But while building the house, I finished the foundation and the first floor. It was a one level house, but it had a hill and a huge basement because the lot had a slope and start for three feet on the front and the back, and the house was about fourteen feet high. I did a big family room in the downstairs because it had a huge foundation and empty place.

My wife's cousin and husband divorced, but both came over and saw that big house I was building. They never came to visit me after because, as I mentioned earlier, they were always jealous. I was not the type of person, but a lot of Hungarians were jealous of what other people had.

His name was Dennis. He did okay, but he was really careful not to work very hard. He was a shoemaker and repaired shoes and boots. He also made some orthopedic shoes. But, he was not really interested in working hard. I stepped into another problem in northern California because Dennis continued to make trouble and gossip in my marriage. I am not going into details into what happened, but to say he just went by there to make a problem and gossip. Dennis had a brother, so these two men went over there. He had a cabin in Lakehead and people came from the Bay Area and had a party. I just continued a sad last day.

I am talking about another very sad thing that happened. My wife always criticized everything that I did wrong. I did wrong another thing. Somebody said do that the wrong way. I said, "What am I doing the wrong way? I make it day by day, plus my son is doing firefighting school in Redding." I said, "Besides, I am building a house."

I lived in and started renting a very nice three-bedroom house before I built a new house. I had a plan to move in the new house. I started working on the house in the fall of '91. All winter it was raining. it was a record rain. 401 inches of rain in Redding and northern California. I was working on a house and finished about 80% and the school I think was finished on June 8th.

On June 9th the whole family went to Hungary. Of course, every year, but for some reason it was that day. At that time, it was the next day they went to Hungary.

I will mention one more example: For some reason, she forgot to ask. She had an excess of money, but for some reason she came to my house and needed money.

I didn't have a cell phone yet. After a couple months, I got my first cell phone, but at this time I didn't have it. She was not too far from the house I was building. She came over and, I don't know, for maybe two, three months she had not come to look at how I was doing on the project and how I far I finished the house. She did not step out of her car and used the horn like, "Hey, I am here."

I went over there. I said, "What you want?"

She said, "I need $100 cash," because she wanted to buy something.

I said, "Okay, I have it," so I gave it to her. But it really made me disappointed. I was building a very nice custom house and then she did not see that for two or three months and was not interested to step out to look at what I was doing. And then my relative was really disappointed also.

So, in '92, it's again just continued family visiting in Hungary. I mostly stayed home, but at that time it was definitely the next day after school finished. And then for some reason they even came back. I don't know. I think they came out on September 3rd and even did not come back to a time when school had started. Even my son lost a little time to start school, and my daughter also. But they did not buy a ticket and at this time even I didn't know exactly why it had happened.

But the house was almost finished and they came back from Hungary and nobody asked me, even the kids. I was a little disappointed they did not come to look at how far I come in finish the house. But the house was almost ready to move in, but I finished about 97%. Slowly I finished it and bought the new furniture and everything and then moved in.

My daughter at this time was in Los Angeles. That was '92. Christmas of '92 she came home. She did not come by airplane; I drove many times. I drove down to Los Angeles because some flights were very long and did not have a very good connection in Los Angeles. To go to Redding, she had to fly to Sacramento and then Sacramento to Redding and they had a very small airplane, and she did not like it very much. She had a problem with her stomach.

For this reason, I took her back to Los Angeles. It was about an eight-hour drive. I had a chance to talk to my daughter and I told her it's okay. Her mom said I was a troublemaker and made things difficult. I was not interested in anything else, just working. But somebody needed to work to make money and put food on the table.

But I was not drinking. I did not have any bad habits. I was raised to working hard; it was sad I was unable to enjoy a life without work. Just work, work, and try to make other people happy or help somebody. But I told my daughter, "Your mom, she has some problems."

She said, "No, no. She's just getting older and has changed her attitude." I said, "okay."

She went back to Los Angeles after finishing a holiday about January 7th. It was a Saturday, and then her school started on Monday about January 9th or 10th. But I don't know why exactly UCLA did not start on January 3rd. It had one-week extra vacation.

I came back to Los Angeles and one evening my wife had a short seizure. It happened on Sunday. On Monday, I took her to a doctor and the doctor checked her.

He said, "Immediately, take her MRI." They took her to MRI. The doctor said, "Well, in a couple days you will have results for what is wrong for you."

On Tuesday they called. She needed to go back on Wednesday at 9 o'clock. She had to talk to a doctor because she had a serious problem. She went back Wednesday at 9 o'clock and then the doctor said she had a brain tumor. We found out she had a tumor in her head, but not cancer. She was born like that and it was even possible as they said my daughter had this type of disease and also my son since it's a genetic.

Her mother had a similar problem because she was forty-seven-year-old and then she always limped her whole life because surgeries had defected her life. She never had a surgery and found out in time. She just took some kind of medicine and stopped the growth. But because it was pushing something in her head, her mother's tumor, she got a limp going a bit. She wasn't walking much. But just that much go back to my mother-in-law.

On Wednesday, a doctor said, "Well, do you guys have health insurance?"

I didn't have health insurance because I had paid the health insurance so for many years until she said, "Why are you paying the health insurance because we do not use it?" She said in Hungary they had free medication and said stop paying Blue Cross insurance.

I made the mistake to said, "Okay, are you serious? You want to drop the health insurance?"

She said, "Yes. Don't pay because we never use it."

I said, "Okay."

I had a beautiful house and a lot. Next lot I started to get the house planning done. I just started building another house by working for a foundation and framing. I said, "Well, I have a house and I have a lot." I decided to sell it. We can see what has happened and how this was going to take care of the medical bill. That one thing was Wednesday and the doctor said she needed surgery this week. I said, "Just we have a chance to sit down and talk about that?"

My son said, "Are you serious? Don't you want to keep my mom alive? You want to kill my mom? The doctor says she needs a surgery now."

I said, "Okay. I am sorry. You got your thing. She needs a surgery now. Go ahead and do it."

Friday, she had a surgery and they took out this tumor. And thank God she survived and came out very well from the surgery. She was in a wheelchair, and then I sold everything and stayed home to take care of her. I sold that house at the last minute, taking care of her because she was in a wheelchair. I was teaching her to walk. I cooked in the house. I cleaned everything.

But she did not change her attitude of fighting about everything. She even hit me with a cane because she was asking me something and I did not answer her. I didn't know what. I answered her question and then she hit me with a cane. But I said, "Sorry. She's just a sick person."

And then I did everything. I took her down to a special doctor to Los Angeles to teach her to walk. But it was a sad thing. She's a nice person, but hardheaded. Again, it was this Dennis saying something or had another Hungarian lady therapist in a Redding hospital. She was always told the opposite of what I recommended.

I read an article in a library and I studied a lot for what surgery she had. I talked to her doctor and other therapist and people were saying how she needed to start to go back to a normal life again.

Even my son said, "You grew up on a farm. You don't know what he's talking about. The therapist definitely knows what she is talking about and her cousin's husband, Dennis."

I said, "Okay, you guys. You do not want to listen to me. I can't change you or anything. You do what you want to do because it doesn't matter what I say. Everything I say is wrong."

I just stayed home and I did everything to help her to go back to a normal life. And thank God, she learned to walk and even got back a driver's license. She was able to drive a car and again I bought for her a very nice Mercedes. She had an Audi before, but it had a lot of miles and I changed the Audi to a Mercedes. And then Audi, it's a very safe car, too. But I said, "Okay."

For some reason, I bought for her a diesel Mercedes, but she really didn't like it because she said a diesel Mercedes was very slow. It's a 300TD, 1985 Mercedes and it was almost in brand-new condition. Somebody used it just a little. I always found a very good deal. Especially Mercedes, because some people had it so many years and used it once in a while. This lady and her husband had a dream to someday have a Mercedes, but she lost it. He was a diabetic and was not driving a car. He had some problems with his vision and he lost his driver's license. And the lady was very old and was unable to drive a car anymore. So, this was why I got the car.

But she was not happy because she said the diesel was very slow.

I said. "Okay. I will change the car." I bought a gas car for her, a Mercedes. My daughter finished UCLA and did an extra year of school. But many times, she used her mom's car or I had one more car many times. Actually, what she drove, a diesel Mercedes, I kept that. My daughter finished school at UCLA and came to Sacramento to stay over there a bit. I bought her a BMW and I tried to do the best for a family.

So, my wife came out nice from surgery. I was suffering again, a problem. She wanted a way to change her life. One time, I was driving my daughter's BMW to Sacramento and something I did to service and tune-up her car and finish fixing a couple things like put in new brake pad, tire. She took down to one other car what I had.

So, after I finished her car, I took it all the way down to Sacramento. I found in a door pocket one tape recorder cassette deck. I put that in the radio and then I found out she went to people reading the future and then she was asking and she tape it what she did there. She was talking about this to a future reader that someday she would find a nice husband or boyfriend. Almost somebody had a dream that someday it's coming — a nice person or somebody who had a Ph.D. But she called a name like somebody. I forget the name.

I said, "Oh, wow. It looks like she's thinking about a way to find somebody and switch me for different person." But it didn't matter how nice she was, what she try to find. But really, I am sure before she was not changing me for a different people because I didn't think anybody would want to take her if somebody saw what her life was like.

So, it came to a point I didn't have it anymore since I sold that big house and I was just renting a house. But I would always rent a very nice house and also had a shop, and a small shop in Redding a small shop. I changed it. I already mentioned it in my book. I have a half acre with a huge shop. I became diabetic. She messed up one man and she wrote me one letter.

She even started fighting with me, "Why did I go home?" I didn't like to fight and then I just went back to the shop even before I saw people were in my house. Even though I didn't like it, I just did so back to the shop. I always had a sleeping bag over there or one Ford when I had it over there. I slept before in a car. But made a place to stay in a Ford van. But then later at that shop, I had a half acre and a very high ceiling shop. I made a studio over there.

In 2002, I separated from my wife because she had a right to live her own life, and she was doing anything she wanted because we were separated. She wrote me this sad letter. In 2002, she went to Hungary and because she returned from Hungary, I rented a very nice a duplex for her. It had an option to buy it. But at this time, I did not buy it, just a lease with an option to buy it. It had rent because I didn't know where things were going and what had happened. But it was a very nice place.

I bought her a very nice Mercedes, what she called an "ambulance car" because in Hungary ambulance cars are white. So just that and then I got diabetes and then the first four or five years I controlled it very well without any serious medicine.

And then Hungarian people came. I tried to help these people. I had a harder time to work because I am diabetic and always I had a lot of work. I made a mistake to hire Hungarian people. I went down many times to the Bay Area and then sometimes to New York to help my niece over there.

I was not always in the shop and she went over there. She found out I was not over there and she went over there in the shop and went through my personal things. She messed up with one Hungarian who came from New York and he much damage over there. I gave it to him to go back to New York, but he never did. I already mentioned it in an early chapter. He moved in her place and because she made more and more of a hard time for me, I was unable to make it through to buy that duplex and just stayed with renting.

The property management called me. It had a problem over there. This man built a gazebo and a swimming pool in the back. She had to move out of this place. And again, I rented a very nice place for her because I thought I didn't want my children sad. So, I was nice to her.

In 2006, the divorce was finalized. But I helped her a lot. Even when we divorced, I left her everything. I did not take anything out from her hand. Only I kept my personal things and the shop. But the only reason I kept the shop was to make money to help my kids and pay her bill because she never worked in her life and didn't know how to make money.

I helped her a lot up to today, because I always said it was my responsibility. I didn't need to legally help her because I left her everything and then I paid her bills all the time. I left her money. She divorced me. I did not take or keep anything for myself, just a shop.

Even in the court, she said, "I would like to make an inventory of the shop and then keep half."

I said, "I will make it much easier." I said it in front of judge and her lawyer. I never hired a lawyer. I protected myself because I did anything she was asking. I said, "Okay, it's yours. Okay, it's yours."

She said she wanted half of the shop.

I said, "I will make it easier. I give it to you, all of it; here's a key and keep it."

She was so disappointed.

Even the judge said, "Are you serious?"

I said, "Yes, I am. I know I need to go someplace and start over." And then it came out when I didn't need to give her anything. So, I gave her zero dollars and zero cents in my whole life. She decided to take this offer and then I left what I had before in many years.

I did work hard in a shop and I made money and still helped to fixing her car. Even she wrecked the car one time. I fixed it for her because she's my kids' mother. I step into a relationship. She gave me a hard time still even not married. Day by day and then I got a girlfriend and she was a very hardworking person and stayed with me over there in a shop in a studio. I brought her over there her car to work on it.

Even my girlfriend cleaned her car and came over there, and actually had restraining order. Finally, she couldn't be allowed to come to my shop. I was not going into all these details because I got already enough sad things, how it's the end of it, my beautiful marriage. And again, I said I worked very hard to keep this marriage, and then I stayed with her in the last minute because I didn't want anyone.

Earlier, even 1989, I almost divorced her. But I said, "No, I'm not going to divorce because I want to raise my children." I said somebody who divorces and has a child and another person has a child has a problem. Why did you do that? Why you did you do that? To your kids? Why do you still talk to your ex-wife? It was here in United States I saw many marriages were over and still contact a husband and wife. Not in my country. Over there, if somebody divorced, it was the end. It was done.

But I am not that type of Hungarian man. I helped her up to today. It even didn't matter what she did to me. I said it was my fault and not hers. I let her stay home and she not did go to finish to her hairstyling school. I knew many hairstylists make pretty good money in the United States, especially my niece in New York. She had been a hairstylist her whole life and she was making $4000 to $6000 a month.

But, I said if you like to stay home, just stay home. It was not necessary. I said, well, probably this was my fault she always stayed home. I did not force her to go to work. But I did not force her to stay home either. So, for some reason, it came out like that.

Again, I did this extra chapter to tell people how hard I worked and how I attempted to keep my marriage. I went to a marriage counselor. We both did. She said she was 150% perfect and I was only 25% perfect.

The marriage counselor said, "If you are talking about it like you are 150% perfect, I don't think I am able to help you."

She wanted to tape what was happening in our marriage counseling. Honestly, I never liked to tape it. But some psychologist was asking about it and then I said I was not happy to have a tape recorder on the side during our marriage counseling session.

The man or woman said, "Ferenc has a right to say no. It means no."

We tried to make marriage counseling work at five different places with another one to never finish even an appointment. Only one man, he charged half hour. The rest of it said, "Even you guys don't pay me anything. Just don't call me anymore and don't make another appointment." And then "thank you" and "nice you showed up" and they just were not interested in doing marriage counseling with us.

But again, it's one marriage where somebody said it's 150% perfect. That way it's a big issue to keep the marriage. In my opinion what I said in beginning of this book, that a husband and wife had to agree to do many things together. Not just a marriage. In a business partnership, or if I am going to go shopping at Home Depot or Walmart, I have to behave over there and follow the rules otherwise they would be calling the police or take me out from a store. First, for a manager, they said it would be better if I left a store because, if not, they were going to call the police.

I saw that in the United States if something was wrong at a house, it's easy to call the police. My opinion is I don't call the police. I just sit down with my partner and make it straight. What was the best way to solve the problem and continue the partnership, marriage, or anything needed to do it, two people together? Otherwise, it's better to split.

What I did was, I divorced her because I was unable to follow what she was doing. She did not listen to me because she said she was 150% perfect and I was only 25%. One more thing I will mention, I went by myself to counseling to figure it out what I needed to do. She had a time to find out what was I did to go to it. It didn't matter how much I hid it. She found out and then gave me a hard time again.

I had special program, a behavioral problem, and it was the same thing with group counseling. I listened to people, what marriage problems other people had, and then I tried to learn from that to save my marriage. I also listened to Dr. Laura and another radio show once a week in Utah. It was a Mormon preacher. He had a lot of people calling in.

I was working very hard to decide and find out how I would be able to keep the marriage. But again, one more time if you are unable to change or calm down your partner – I am a Catholic – it was better just to divorce because it could ruin a kid's life, and then it wasn't worth it.

But again, when stepping into a new relationship or new partner, you had to take a chance and accept a new partner might have a child too. It was hard to keep a marriage together because everything was much harder in life than it used to be, and it still had a solution to keep the marriage going. Both people had to listen to their partner and not judge their partner all the time.

Again, I am not perfect. Of course, I am not. Every day I learn and try to find out which way is the best to do something, and then have a nice day. I have beautiful children. I have beautiful grandkids. I said life is too short. Better go that way.

Chapter 13

Advice for Marriage

I would like to start this chapter to tell someone who has been through the same situation I have that they aren't alone. I would like to explain why I was unable to keep this beautiful marriage forever.

I built my marriage up. I mentioned how I met my wife: I had my first date and my first girlfriend for close to two years. Something definitely happened, as she needed to go to Yugoslavia. My sister had a wedding on the same day and I met another girl. We played together as kids and then I did not see her for ten years. She was a beautiful girl, but that was not a reason to change my relationship with her because I didn't like Julie. I loved her and I liked her. We had an amazing time. But, for some reason. it happened that way. It meant it was not just a relationship with somebody.

A lot of people have had, for some reason, a good business or marriage and, in one way or another, never knew why it made a problem in a marriage. I was raised hard, but I saw \ my parents were never really fighting. They had miscommunications, but they always smoothly took care of the problem. But one thing I knew my mother never said was, "I want to do it a different way because my neighbor or my friend or somebody said what you're doing is wrong."

Many marriages – I think I used these words earlier in the chapter – have to accept somebody in the way they were raised or accept their habits or person or things.

I said to never push another person to do it their own way. They have to do it to see how it's done and talk nicely if there is a problem. But I saw how my parents raised me and told me what I needed to do, and I was never thinking about why I needed to do it probably because I was raised that way.

I grew up and then had a relationship with Julie. I saw she read my mind and tried to find out what I liked best and what was good for me. I did it the same way, but immediately found out she was working to make the relationship smooth and nice. I mean, this was not hard for her because she was raised that way. Making her happy and doing nice things for her was not hard for me because there was an atmosphere where I loved her and was 100% sure to use that word — that she loved me, too.

But, for some reason. it happened that way. She had to go to Yugoslavia. For some reason, I had to meet a girl I had not seen in almost ten years. People gossiped and changed her mind. I do not blame Marta; I am using her name now. She was really the one reason. Nobody knew what the reason was to intrude my relationship with Julie.

I was not the only person who had people gossiping about me and causing a problem for another person. Again, it didn't matter if it was a business partner or a marriage because a marriage didn't just mean engagement. Marriage had a wedding ring and an engagement ring, and people went before the public in ceremony to become husband and wife.

That other had to work together with a business — day-by-day, good thing/bad thing — because everybody had a hard time and a good time. They had to do it together. It had a nice thing and they had to help each together to solve the problem if something was wrong. Number one — never, ever blame another person. Not just because I was raised with my mother blaming me for mostly everything in the house because I was not her favorite son, and I accepted it. I never judged my mom. I never thought about why she did it or why she wasn't doing the same to my sister.

The reason I mentioned it was because I stepped into a new relationship. The way she saw something was she found out something about my personality, and I was sure she liked it. I honestly – because I had a relationship – didn't want to make her fight in beginning to start to change my mind to dating with her. But in my first relationship, I was working hard to keep it and continue it. But Julie, for some reason, stayed away from me and did not accept my offer to continue a nice relationship anymore.

Just to mention it a little bit: I had my half-brother. He had a similar situation. He took a three-year term as a soldier in Hungary and he had a girlfriend. Actually, this was not just a girlfriend, but a fiancé who was waiting for him to finish a three-year army term. That might have happened in 1956, and he was supposed to finish his term in the spring of '51 and then marry her.

But his girlfriend changed her mind and then messed up with my half-brother's cousin. They had an extremely nice relationship and then it became sadder. His cousin was the best friend of my half-brother, but he took away his fiancé and they got married instead.

But first, since I did it a little too fast, my brother came home because there was a civil war in Hungary. So, then he went to that one in 1957. On Easter, he went to her house on Sunday and then they went to a dancing place. I heard about it when I was only seven years old. It did not go very well that day. He met her and the next day he went because, in Hungary, Easter is two days. The next day, he went to her house and she gave him back an engagement ring.

It was hard. He had so many things that hurt his life and heart because, in an innocent way, somebody made hard time for with communism. Just a little bit on everything and then also he was a very big, but not a strong, person. He easily got hurt if something happened to him.

She gave back the engagement ring. I will never forget when he came home on Monday afternoon, which was the second day of Easter. He always liked me very much. He put me on his knee and was extremely nice. He had a nice voice and sang to me one song. I saw his eyes. A tear came out, but I was just a kid and I didn't know what had happened. He hugged me and I will never forget. He gave me twenty forints. In my country, the money is forint. He was holding me tightly and he cried and I just didn't know what had happened.

The next morning – we found out that evening – he drank a strong poison. The reason he came home that afternoon was to say goodbye to the family, give a hug to mostly everybody, and that evening he committed suicide. My father was hurt badly. My mother was just his stepmother, but she was hurt badly, too. His sister was, too. So, everybody missed him very badly.

The reason I mention this is because there are many different relationships, and for some reason, one way or the other, they do not always work out, and a lot of people choose to commit suicide.

I already had so many sad things from what I have seen, and not just my half-brother's story. I heard about many other similar situations because the relationship did not work out. It would be where one girl or a boy would commit suicide to solve the sad thing.

I said myself that love in the relationship came in a person's own heart and then to make one relationship work nicely, both need to work hard to make it happen and continue the relationship. Again, at least in the world today, nobody was perfect. Everybody had some problem or good thing, bad thing, and nice thing. Or something happened to make it automatically, or it meant they had a bad day and did nothing, and then another beautiful day happened.

Many times, when something happened or something went wrong, I have said to try to work on it and still unable to make it happen to work. I have said that it can start to make it clear some miscommunication or problem because somebody would say something. Again, this would be gossip.

I have said I wanted to listen my wife's or my partner's story. Sometimes, even though I disagree with what my partner said and start to think about the way they're mad, I don't think I have the right answer. I don't want to step in to stop my partner to say, "No way. You're wrong. I know what I'm doing, and what I say is right." I always say it's better to wait one day or two to give some time for a partner to get a right answer.

I never forgot. One time I went into 7-11 store and parked my car and saw that one car had taken two parking spots. He did not even park his car straight. Then, I went in the 7-11 waiting in line to pay. It came time to go to the cash register to buy gas and a snack. One man ran into the store yelling and used a bad name for this person because there were no other parking spots, and somebody took two parking spots.

One person was on the phone and then he asked me and another person, "Are you," again using the name, "take those two spots?"

The man had to hold on, put his hand on the phone, and said, "I'm sorry, man. But I parked wrong."

He went over to the man and pushed and yelled at him.

He finished his conversation on the phone and said, "Sorry, man, I took up two parking spots. I was in a hurry because my wife is very sick and I don't have a phone at home and had to call an ambulance."

This is the reason I mention many times why people need to wait and find out why something happened before they start losing patience.

To continue it, Julie did not ask for my excuse or explain to her what had happened. I didn't need to apologize to her as to why I stayed at a wedding with Marta. She would not listen to me. I said I lost, too. But she lost something, too, and would find out in the future.

She went in, but not immediately. Of course, because she found out I accepted her personal thing she did not want to accept my love anymore. worked hard one way or another way to make it happen to continue it. But she did not listen to me and had another strong person step into my life and there was a lot of hurt. I had my kid's life and I saw Marta's situation and thought about it. It looked like God wanted it that way; to continue the relationship with her.

One more story on what happened to Julie. She stayed away from me and, not immediately, she stepped in another relationship with somebody. She got one really bad person, an alcoholic, and he beat her and so many times. I would never say that it was God punishing her. God is not punishing anybody. For some people, things happened; I did not say exactly that they did it by themselves. But before choosing something, they need to think about it or even don't know they might step out of some good thing and never know they are stepping into a bad thing. For some reason, for everybody something can happen for some reason.

Pretty quickly, Marta and I realized both of us needed to start a new life and we decided to get married in the next year. But Julie and I had a plan to do the same. Of course, when she found out, I seriously stepped out and took her out of my heart because, for me, it did not work overnight. I was suffering for that. I did not hide that for a couple of years. But, I mean, at first in my marriage, Marta was so nice to me and was working very hard to make the marriage work because she had a problem with her brother and so many other things happened in the house. She thought about it. I was, for her, a strong man and a strong partner to help continue her peaceful life. And we did okay.

I am going to start from the beginning. I found out, even after being married for a couple of months, that we had different personalities. I was raised on a farm. She was raised in a city. But again, I worked extremely hard to make it happen to accept what were her favorite things and what she liked. I accepted what she didn't like and did not push her to going my own way. My way to something happening if I saw it was another person was happy. That one in the beginning worked very well and everything was so nice. Of course, in a short time she got pregnant and delivered her first child.

When she delivered the first one, her mother gave an apology and accepted my marriage and she accepted me. I worked very hard to continue a nice relationship with my parents. I brought my children over there. I was working very hard to get a chance and at the time to bring my children to my parents' house because I wanted to raise my children to know who their grandpa and grandma were. My parents were not interested much, but I accepted that and still wanted my children to know their paternal grandparents.

On Marta's side, my children's grandpa did not care very much for his daughter, his granddaughter, or for me, but I accepted it. I did not blame Marta for her father. I never liked to do it to somebody and say, "Why do you have that type of father or why do you that type of friend who is not nice to me?" Either I meet somebody and they are nice to me and I accept it, or they try to give me a hard time and I don't need to accept them and stay away from that person to not make him happy if a person makes me a hard time.

In Hungary, I let her stay home to raise the kids, and there were not many battles. There were also other women raising their kids who did not need to go to work every day. She always had a friend come to the house to drink coffee. I had a pretty good job because I was working for Steve in auto repair and was able to make everything nice in a house. She was lucky to get a person to work hard to make a nice home, and I was lucky in the same way to find a person who liked what I was doing and happy to stay with me.

However, if it was somebody's birthday or another kind of party, I did not go because I was raised not knowing how I to do it. Sometimes I did, but really it did not make a difference to her if I went to a party or not. She was raised in a city in a totally different way. She enjoyed it in a different way to think how I thought to enjoy it to go to a party.

Even when I went to some party or my brother's or a friend's house to go to party, I was not drinking and didn't have a thing to talk about because I didn't know them and they were totally thinking in a different way and talking about different stories. I didn't know what they were talking about. Mostly, I spent the time with the kids or in a house and fixed a TV antenna, fixed a TV, or fixed a washer/dryer or not a dryer, just a washer because there were no dryers in Hungary and then always just something or I would play with the kids.

But I didn't have any comments to share with another person because many people were gossiping. For example: "I knew he did it – that and that and that." I never wanted to hear about it and never really liked to gossip about somebody's life. I always said that life was too short and when I had a little time, I spent the time with my sweet children or my wife, or my friend who was interested in my company. So, I did it that way.

Of course, I had a hard time with my mother-in-law. It didn't matter if she was happy to see my marriage or she needed help. There's a bit of a story. I tried to help her, and she was the type of person where it didn't matter what I was doing for her.

She said, "That way I like what you did," number one for her, "Why are that and that like that? Why don't you do it another way?"

As an example: she had a house and shared a fence with a neighbor, and the fence for ten, fifteen years had garbage over there. I cleaned the garbage, cleaned and fixed and built a new fence. I made everything nicely and everything was done. I did it using cedar wood, and she didn't want to paint cedar with paint, but only using linseed oil to stain it.

She said, "Ferenc, it's okay I have this fence, but why aren't the boards not the same color? Why are some darker? Why are some lighter?"

I said, "Oh, oh, well, if you need more trees from a forest growing like that one that's a little lighter. I see that one it's a little darker and has a tree own design, I did not do it."

Because she had a boutique and I helped her make more successful and her son of course as I already mentioned earlier was her favorite boy. There was a county fair. I bought my own tent to have a thing to go to a county fair to sell at the county fair kids' toys and balloons and everything to make a little extra money. I did it pretty well a couple times.

I said, "Well, I don't want you to make yourself reach in my license but I going to accept that even what I made in money I will give it to her half of one and I will use my money to buy toys."

She said, "How about my son? He has to go to the county fair next weekend. I would like it if he could use your tent and your material."

He said did it, but, he did not really do it. My wife's brother did it. He had an extremely hardworking, nice wife. She controlled it to go to make more money because my wife's brother was a very handsome boy, but he didn't know how to work and was not interested in working.

What happened at the county fair was it had a big thunderstorm and everything got wet. They came home and my mother-in-law had a basement and these people had put it over there all the toys and the tent. They just dropped it over there and then left it over there. I waited one day to organize it, and said, "Thank you, Ferenc. And sorry it has happened."

I stopped going to make it to happen to a county fair. Not because I got upset. Again, my mother-in-law went a negative way.

I said, "Okay, you're thinking about how I am using you, and I did not get upset." I just said, "Okay, let me know what day your son can make a way on how I can give it to them and then I will be ready to go again to the county fair." And then it never happened.

She died a couple years ago, and then my family and my son went back to Hungary after twenty years. It's the same, everything over in that corner, how he did it twenty years ago. So, it's another thing just a bit the same thing. My parents had a ranch and then after 1975 I brought electricity to my farm. I helped to get the electricity for my parent's house because my farm was next to them.

I helped get power to his house and there used to be that drinking water – already I mentioned it – was about a half a mile from my house. I made a special valve to pump the water and an electric motor to have water go inside a building, and just needed to turn on the faucet and my parents had the water.

I did it, but my mother was never happy what I did, and said, "Well, now you are happy you don't need to go over there anymore with a bucket to pick up water; you are coming here and turn the water into drinking water."

I said, "No, Mom. I did it for you and my father, too. Because you are not young anymore. And now you guys have water inside the house."

I made it happen to having a wood burning water heater to make water to take a shower. I did not make a bathtub, just a shower, because I always liked to do something to make another person happy. But I did something and my parents did not like it or were not happy, I was still happy to do it.

I never wanted to change my parents. I accepted how they raised me and how they were nice to me or bad to me. I use these words "nice to me" because it was sad, but it didn't really happen that way. The only way I was able to use "nice to me" was what I did to my parents to accept it. This was what would make me happy. They did not say "thank you" or they were glad to have it. It was they just let me do it. But it's the way I accepted it and the way I grew up.

In Hungary, there were bad people and they tried to ruin my beautiful marriage, and there were jealous people over my two beautiful children. I bought some toys for the children but didn't go crazy to buy them. Even my mother-in-law, or my kid's grandma, had a boutique. Still, I did not let them to bring home all kinds of junk to a house.

I made it happen to do some kind of work to play with handwriting something or a natural way to bring my daughter to my farm. My son did not like it and was not interested to come, and my wife did not really want him to come to a farm. But again, I accepted it. I was never pushing her to come to my farm.

Sometimes somebody would be doing something because this was the way they would like to do it and to change a person's mind, it sometimes would just step into a problem. It did not mean I spent all the time apologizing or myself feel like I had a hard time to make my partner or my wife happy. I just didn't want to fight in front of the kids and did not take it seriously that she was acting like that way and then she was going to ruin my life. No. Because I loved her and I loved her that way.

So again, still the marriage went well in Hungary, even though not only one person was trying to make a hard time or make gossip for her. I was in the farming business and auto repair business and I had an offer. Some women were nice to me, especially when they knew how I raised my children. A woman had an extremely difficult life in a home and not just one. It was many of them who had husbands who would go to a bar and drink hard and beat their wives very badly. It was a lot of women were looking for something to escape or change her own life. But I am not the type of person to chase a woman.

I helped or gave advice on how they would be able to manage her own life, but not really try to step in to ruin somebody's marriage. And then what has happened in Hungary a little bit. Even though she never drank, or smoked, she started to see a couple things a different way. But again, I did not take it seriously. I did not want to do it to put it on the table or sit down and talk about why it was happening or why you do it. I just tried to find out a way to accept what she did.

There were many reasons but especially my mother. I already put in the book what she did for my business and my youngest brother and in a school how my daughter had a problem with a teacher and a teacher started to make a hard time for my son. I made it serious. For a long time, I was thinking about someday going to the United States. I already had this in my chapter in my book.

At that time, I did not put that over there in my book that yes, I came to the United States in 1975 to see what the next step would be to change my life to make sure I was not going to make a mistake to bring my family to the United States. At this time, everything came out very well. I saw this was a beautiful country, and then I was talking to people and I found out if somebody was working hard and know why they were working hard. But nobody would care how many cars I had or how nice a house I had or how many houses I had.

I went back and that was in my chapter before. I did not mention that in 1975 I went back to Hungary. The next year in 1976, before I started any farming or really doing big things to do it, bigger to choose it to stay in Hungary, I went to Yugoslavia to try to bring my family to the United States.

The reason I mentioned it at this time in the chapter probably did not mean it started a marriage problem. I started to see what my wife was doing, and then in Yugoslavia I accepted a chance to immigrate to the United States.

My wife started to cry, "Well, I think I changed my mind. I would like to go back to Hungary to continue life over there because I miss my grandpa." At that time her grandpa was still alive. She missed her mother and a friend and so many things.

The reason I mentioned it was that one was a very big step to leave Hungary. At this time, I had been working hard. I had a lot of friends, too. But I was not involved in a very big project. What I did had already in some project but not worth it to stay in that country if it has a lot of hurt in my family. That one was at that time my son was only just one year old. My daughter was three years old.

She saw she was not happy and it did not work out. Again, I tried to do it her own way to make her happy and I didn't want to start in a new life with another country and she was not happy and did not have parents or family or friend.

I said, "Okay, you want to go back." And we went back.

I am not going into details, but just a little bit. I had my half-sister's son. He came with me in 1976 and he did not change his mind. He stayed in Yugoslavia. He immigrated to the United States. But one way or another, the government found out I tried to immigrate to the United States. I received a harsh punishment, but again, I said I have to accept it.

I worked hard and continued working hard in Hungary. I had tons of friends and jobs to do it. I decided my wife was happy and wanted to stay in my own country. She could go ahead and do it. But besides that, God showed it to her look at what has happened to your daughter in a school and what had happened our son. What her mother was doing to her husband and she knew how hard I was working and I never hurt my parents or my brother. She knew I always was working very hard to make another person happy.

Other things followed because I had more and more money. I had a bigger house, and then she came up and said:

"Ferenc, I realize how much damage I did to you and how hard you're working and people are always mean to you. You think it's good I try to immigrate to the United States?" I have a feeling it has to be to put that in a story and in my book.

I started working to do it seriously plus somebody made the fire on my farm in 1983 and I got the penalty from the government. My mother and I had my brother, youngest brother, step into our lives. For this reason, I decided to immigrate to the United States on August 17, 1983.

I had put a bit that in 1980 that the first time I stopped in Austria was very sad. Even in Austria, there were more immigrant families and she started acting different way. She got a little bit bossy and said, "Ferenc, that one is wrong. You're thinking wrong." And she did not before that.

I said, "Will you accept it again?" Well, because we left so many things in Hungary from what she had in a house."

She had friends, but honestly, she did not have a strong relationship and even her own mother was jealous of her for what life she has. I am not talking about how much jealousy many other people felt or my two brother's wives were jealous of her. She would stay home and raise kids.

Not just my brother's wife, but a lot of women had to work extremely hard and put food on a table and take care of the home. They did everything to make it happen to organize a kitchen, a house, a shirt, and everything because not one husband made a dinner in Hungary. A wife would work like a slave and had to make everything in a house straight. And a husband, almost 100%, went in a house and just dropped a boot or a shirt at front of a door or whatever. But they never knew how they needed to clean a table or make some day-by-day food on the table.

Yes, they worked hard to make money to pay the bills, but not interested in doing kitchen work or anything in a home. Hungary was a little different, unlike here in the United States or many other places. In Austria, husbands took life easy over there. It's really the wife who's like a slave working on the farm and the barn and all over. The husband was drinking in a bar.

I said, "Okay, no problem." I came to the United States and then she was unhappy in New York. And that did not mean in Hungary did not have mild winters or cold winters. There step in a very interesting cold winter in New York. Plus, we had always lived in a private house. We had not lived in an apartment. We lived in a condominium, but a condominium in Hungary was like a private house and nice and peaceful. Plus, there were no cockroaches. Kids were unhappy, so I accepted my wife was not happy over there; she called and found out in very short time her cousin in California.

I got an extremely good job. I am not going into it as already did on the details. A changed my mind. It did not mean I said it was always my dream to go to the United States. I liked to start my life in New York, New York. But she did not like it and she wanted to go to California. I said okay. Number one for me was to make my family happy, so I did.

Even in California, a job was not waiting for me. I worked in a wrecking yard for minimum wage. In New York, I made more than three times that money. It had a person, an owner of the business, who spoke my own language, and I spoke some German because the business owner in New York was from Germany and a Hungarian owned it. I didn't have a hard time working, and in California I stepped in the next day a hard time I saw that. But again, she liked it and wanted it that way.

I said, "Okay, I will work and not blame her." I thought about going by myself back to New York to make extra money to start someplace nicer place in California, and I learn more English. God helped me in my life and my family to go down to Monterey, a beautiful, beautiful, beautiful place. It was one of the nicest in the world. It was the nicest and best climate to live.

I met somebody in New York who was looking for poppy seed and then she was talking to me and became a nice friend immediately. But I had this gift from God and it's my nature. It did not matter where I was. All the time, I found a good friend and a nice person to work with, and then again of course there have been bad people. I was not unhappy to see that and try to make a hard time for me. But I was always ready to accept and make a step to stop a person what is trying to do for me a hard time.

But I know I did not change my mother's mind, and I didn't want to change her mind in regards to my youngest brother. Because she did it, I did not want to stay in Hungary. So, I made a beautiful place and lived my family in northern California. So, I kept my family in northern California and I was in this beautiful Monterey. I made a beautiful small house to move over there.

I did not move over there in a little barn or not comfortable place. And then the place was even nice.

I already had a feeling to change my marriage. She was bossier and more often said that somebody say that. But the biggest, biggest, biggest problem was that she was homesick to Hungary. But this happened only in the beginning. After first visiting Hungary, she found out I did not make a mistake bringing the whole family to the United States. She didn't have a chance going back to Hungary. I'm not going to try to explain how hard of a time and how many days I had because she did that.

I already mentioned it. I immediately stared to make pretty nice money because I found immediately a nice person to help me make good money. In November of 1984, her mother visited my house in Monterey. She stayed over and was so happy to see how nice a place I made for a family. Because she was homesick, her mom went home and I bought the ticket for her. A lot of cousins came over with a husband to visit and tried to make her happy. And then in the spring of '86, her brother came over there, even though she did not have a very good relationship with her brother.

What was more interesting was what I say now. She was not really here. And here she did not see her father. In about August of '87, her father came to the United States, and her visit did not go very well. But her father and I had many, many nice days. He came to my shop. He came while I was working on construction. He came with me everywhere. He was amazed what I was doing for a family.